21ST CENTURY READING

CREATIVE THINKING AND READING WITH TEDTALKS

Laurie Blass – Jessica Williams – Colleen Sheils

NATIONAL GEOGRAPHIC LEARNING | **CENGAGE Learning**

Australia • Brazil • Japan • Korea • Mexico • Singapore • Spain • United Kingdom • United States

**21st Century Reading Teacher's Guide 4
Creative Thinking and Reading with
TED Talks**

Laurie Blass

Jessica Williams

Colleen Sheils

Publisher: Andrew Robinson

Executive Editor: Sean Bermingham

Development Editor: Christopher Street

Director of Global Marketing: Ian Martin

Product Marketing Manager: Anders Bylund

Media Researcher: Leila Hishmeh

Director of Content and Media Production:
  Michael Burggren

Production Manager: Daisy Sosa

Senior Print Buyer: Mary Beth Hennebury

Cover and Interior Designer:
  Brenda Carmichael

Cover Image: ©James Duncan Davidson/TED

Composition: SPi Global

For permission to use material from this text or product, submit all requests online at **cengage.com/permissions**

Further permissions questions can be emailed to
permissionrequest@cengage.com

Teachers Guide
ISBN 13: 978-1-305-26634-6

National Geographic Learning/Cengage Learning
20 Channel Center Street
Boston, MA 02210
USA

Cengage Learning is a leading provider of customised learning solutions with office locations around the globe, including Singapore, the United Kingdom, Australia, Mexico, Brazil and Japan. Locate our local office at **international.cengage.com/region**

Cengage Learning products are represented in Canada by Nelson Education Ltd.

Visit National Geographic Learning online at **NGL.Cengage.com**
Visit our corporate website at **www.cengage.com**

Printed in the United States of America
Print Number: 03   Print Year: 2017

CONTENTS

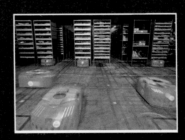

UNIT WALKTHROUGH

21st Century Reading develops core academic language skills and incorporates 21st Century themes and skills such as global awareness, information literacy, and critical thinking.

Each unit of the Student Book has three parts:

- **Lesson A:** Students read about a 21st Century topic.
- **Lesson B:** Students view a TED Talk which expands upon the topic in Lesson A.
- **Project:** Students explore the topic further by completing a collaborative research project.

1

Each unit begins with an outline of the learning goals.

2

Think and Discuss questions help to raise learners' interest in the unit theme and activate prior knowledge.

3

Lesson A focuses on a reading passage that provides background and context for the TED Talk in Lesson B.

4

Pre-reading activities introduce key terms and content that learners will encounter in the reading passage, and develop previewing skills such as skimming and making predictions.

5 **Infographics**, including maps, captions, charts, and graphs, develop learners' visual literacy—their ability to decode graphic information effectively.

6 Reading texts are accompanied by glossaries to aid comprehension of lower frequency items that students may be unfamiliar with.

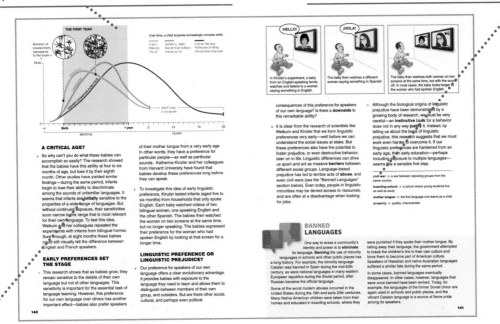

7 Useful academic words and phrases are highlighted in bold and provide the basis for vocabulary building activities later in the lesson.

8 Reading skill tasks focus on key reading strategies such as identifying main and supporting ideas, and understanding cause/effect relationships.

9 Post-reading tasks incorporate graphic organizers, such as sketch maps, Venn diagrams, and timelines in order to help students visualize and understand key concepts.

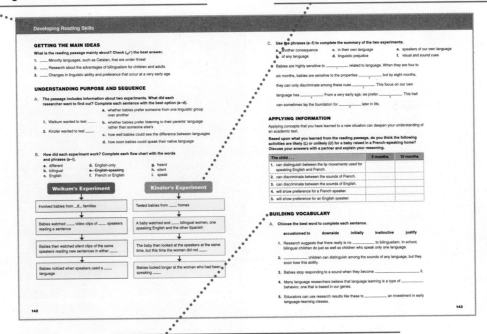

10 Vocabulary building tasks focus on the academic words and phrases highlighted in the passage. All target vocabulary is listed at the back of the student book.

11 **Meaning from Context** tasks help learners to understand idiomatic and colloquial expressions.

12 **Critical Thinking** questions encourage students to analyze, evaluate, and apply ideas to their own experience, as well as synthesizing ideas from the reading and the talk.

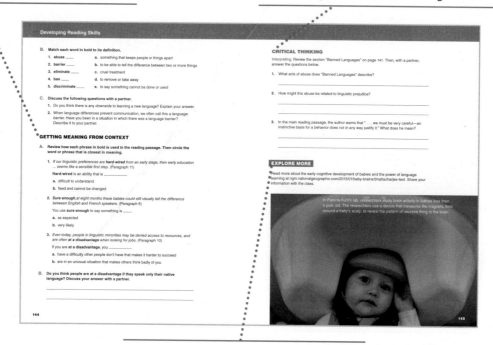

13 **Explore More** sections provide suggestions for further reading or viewing—such as related TED Talks and National Geographic articles.

14 **Lesson B** focuses on the key ideas in a TED Talk that relate to the overall unit theme.

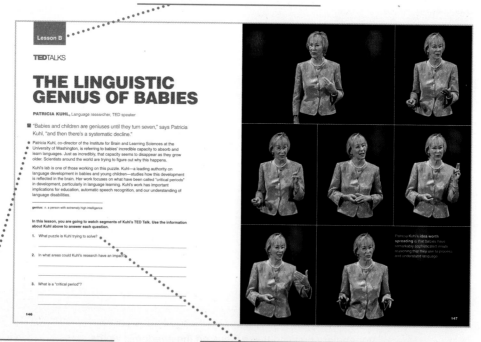

15 A short reading passage provides background information about the speaker.

16 Comprehension questions check students' understanding of the speaker's background.

17 A previewing task typically features a short excerpt from the TED Talk together with questions helping students to predict the main theme.

18 The adapted TED Talks are often divided into two parts, each with associated activities. These parts are also noted in the video transcripts at the back of the Student Book.

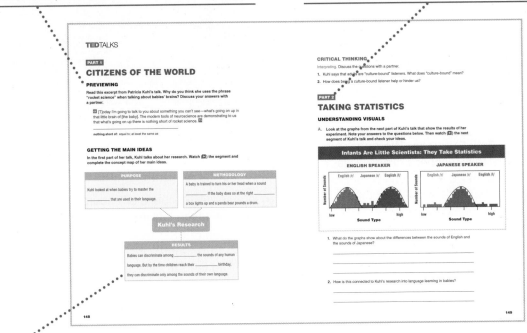

19 A range of visuals are incorporated to summarize key points of the talk and also to preview subject-specific terminology.

20 Guided comprehension tasks focus on the speaker's main ideas, and language he/she uses to convey those ideas.

21 Each unit concludes with a project-based activity which brings together ideas from the unit in a productive task.

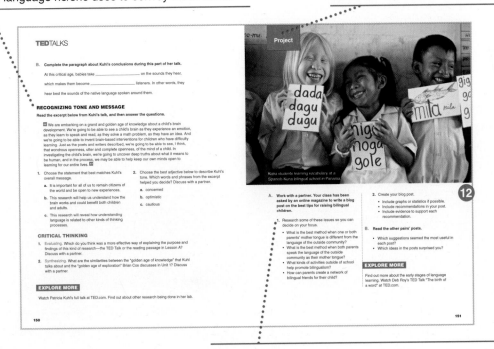

22 Projects take the form of research assignments, short presentations, interviews, etc. The Teacher's Guide provides advice for teachers in terms of structuring the project and also suggests functional language to pre-teach before students begin the task.

Series Components

An **Audio CD** features narrations of each reading passage and TED speaker profile. These are highlighted by a ( ) icon in the Student Book.

A **DVD** accompanying the series contains each adapted TED Talk. Each talk can also be viewed online (visit NGL.Cengage.com/21centuryreading). Viewing activities are highlighted by a ( ) icon in the Student Book.

A photocopiable **TED Talk Summary Worksheet** is provided on page 10 of this Teacher's Guide. This can be used to aid students' comprehension of the TED Talks featured in the Student Book, or those recommended as extension activities.

Annotated Video Transcripts for each TED Talk can be found on pages 71–95 of this Teacher's Guide. These provide explanations of language items and cultural references that may be unfamiliar to students.

Other components in the series include:

• an interactive Student eBook

• an interactive Teacher's eResource that can be used as a presentation tool in class

• an **Assessment CD-ROM** containing ExamView® question banks for teachers who want to create customized tests or give students additional language practice

WELCOME TO 21ˢᵀ CENTURY READING!

Globalization and the internet are changing the way students learn. Today's young adult and adult ESL/EFL learners need to develop not only core academic English skills such as reading, viewing, and vocabulary skills, but also essential global and cross-cultural awareness, creative and critical thinking skills, and information and media literacies.

In **21ˢᵗ Century Reading**, motivating speakers and innovative content from TED—and its focus on **ideas worth spreading**—provide an exciting opportunity to inspire learners as they develop these essential skills.

The main objective of **21ˢᵗ Century Reading** is to enable learners to understand and respond to ideas and content in English, by reading articles adapted for level and viewing related TED talks. The focus is on the key ideas of each text and talk—and the language that the writer or speaker uses to convey those ideas. In most cases, the TED Talk has been abridged to focus on two or three segments that best represent the speaker's key ideas.

As learners progress through the series, they develop essential reading and vocabulary skills, such as scanning quickly for specific information, making connections between main and supporting ideas, and inferring meaning from context. In addition, learners are encouraged to think critically about each text and TED talk, for example by:

- **Analyzing** an article or excerpt in detail in order to identify key points and arguments.
- **Evaluating** evidence to decide how credible, relevant, or sufficient the information is.
- **Reasoning** and justifying solutions to a problem, based on logical conclusions.
- **Inferring** what a writer or speaker is saying indirectly, and interpreting figurative language.
- **Synthesizing** ideas from more than one source in order to make a judgment or conclusion.
- **Predicting** what will happen, either later in the text or at a future time.
- **Reflecting** on a writer's/speaker's ideas and applying those ideas to other contexts.

We hope that you—and your students—enjoy your journey through **21ˢᵗ Century Reading**, and that along the way you discover many ideas worth spreading!

Name: _____ Class: _____

TED Talk Summary Worksheet

Unit: _____ Video Title: _____

Speaker: _____

What information do you learn about the speaker and his/her background?

_____

_____

_____

Summarize the main idea of the talk in one sentence.

_____

What supporting details or examples does the speaker use to support his/her idea?

_____

_____

_____

How does the speaker engage the audience? For example, using images, charts, humor, actions, etc.

_____

_____

_____

What is your opinion of the talk? What words or phrases would you use to describe it?

_____

_____

_____

What language in the video was new to you? Make a note of three words or phrases that the speaker used. Write a sentence or definition for each one.

_____

_____

_____

WHY EXPLORE?

UNIT OVERVIEW

Reading: Students read about the human instinct to explore.

TED Talk: Scientist Brian Cox talks about the need for curiosity-driven science and exploration.

Project: Students give a presentation about everyday technology developed as a result of space exploration.

 **Lesson 1A** **THE URGE TO EXPLORE**

LESSON OVERVIEW

Aims:
- Read and comprehend an article discussing theories about why humans have the urge to explore.
- Get the main ideas.
- Identify supporting information.
- Make inferences.

Target Vocabulary: acquire, authority, consult, encounter, innately, obsessed with, prospect, solely, variant, visionary

Reading Passage Summary: Students read about humanity's history of exploration and why we are compelled to discover new places. Even before the Age of Exploration, which defined our modern map of the world, humans have been setting out to find new lands. Perhaps it is in the genetic makeup of humans to have this instinct to explore. Research has identified genes that possibly give us a foundational sense of curiosity and restlessness that pushes us to explore. While we have already explored much of our own planet, technology is now allowing us to go into the universe beyond.

TEACHING NOTES

THINK AND DISCUSS

This unit talks about the human instinct to explore, why we have it, and how it drives us. Have students discuss their answers to the questions in pairs first. Then elicit a class discussion on places that are left to explore both on Earth and beyond. *Extension:* Have the class brainstorm a list of adjectives to describe how an explorer discovering a new place for the first time might feel.

PRE-READING

A. Note that the pictures represent two different ages of exploration: past and present. Ask students to think about how exploration has changed over the years and what the differences and similarities are between explorations hundreds (or thousands) of years ago and now. Have students discuss with a partner. Elicit ideas

Think and Discuss

1. Answers will vary. Possibilities include: space and the universe, the Earth's oceans at great depths. **2.** Answers will vary.

Pre-reading

A. Answers will vary. Both pictures show small ships exploring vast areas. While the location and mode of transport have changed, in many ways the motivation and reasons for exploring are still the same. We want to find new places, learn new things, and experience both the adventure and challenge of doing this.

B. 1. The adjective *restless* describes a state of not being able to stay still or inactive. Guesses will vary about the meaning of "restless genes." The heading refers to the possibility that the restless nature of humans, which pushes us to explore, may be part of our genetic makeup.; **2.** Guesses will vary. The heading refers to exploring beyond our planet, to space and the universes beyond.; **3.** Answers will vary. The phrase suggests that the desire to explore has always existed—and will always exist—in humans.

Getting the Main Ideas

A. Section 1: a; **Section 2:** c; **Section 3:** b

B. b

Identifying Supporting Information

A 1. c, e; **2.** b, f; **3.** a, d

B. 1. curiosity; **2.** Humans have a long childhood, during which we are dependent on our parents. This allows us to focus less on survival and more on developing our intelligence through curiosity driven exploration.; **3.** The brain development that happens during childhood gives us the tools needed to explore effectively as adults. We take risks, test out possibilities and strategies, and challenge ourselves to make accomplishments like landing a rover on Mars.

Making Inferences

A. 1. b; **2.** b; **3.** a

B. Answers will vary.

Building Vocabulary

A. 1. visionary; **2.** obsessed with; **3.** prospect; **4.** encountered; **5.** consult

B. 1. b; **2.** d; **3.** a; **4.** c; **5.** a

C. 1. Answers will vary.; **2.** Answers will vary. Possibilities include: language abilities, social skills, a sense of humor.

Getting Meaning from Context

1. b; **2.** a; **3.** a; **4.** b

Critical Thinking

Answers will vary.

---

from students, making a Venn diagram on the board to show the similarities and differences.

B. Give students a minute to skim the title, headings, and introduction. Note that the questions require students to make guesses and inferences about meaning by examining terms picked up while skimming. Check answers as a class. For question 1, tell students to look at the components of the word *restless* in order to understand its meaning. Check answers as a class.

DEVELOPING READING SKILLS

GETTING THE MAIN IDEAS

A. Have students read the entire passage, either silently or while listening to the narrated passage on the audio. Have them identify the main points

individually before checking answers as a class. Elicit the information in the passage that helped them find the correct answers.

B. Have students work individually to complete the activity before checking answers in pairs. ***Extension:*** Ask students to discuss in pairs whether or not they agree with the main idea of the passage. Tell them to support their opinions with examples and reasons.

IDENTIFYING SUPPORTING INFORMATION

A. Have students work individually to complete the activity. Note that each section has two supporting details. Check answers as a class. Go back to **Getting the Main Ideas** to connect each supporting detail with the overall idea of the section. Ask students to comment on how the details support the main idea.

B. Ask students to identify what part of the passage the question is referring to (the sidebar). Encourage partners to answer the questions together and then discuss their thoughts and opinions about each one.

MAKING INFERENCES

A. Review the meaning of "making inferences" with students. Make sure students understand that it's about reading between the lines, and understanding meaning that is not directly stated. Ask them to identify what can help them to make inferences about meaning: information given, word choice used, author's tone. Have students work individually or in pairs to complete the activity before checking answers.

B. Tell pairs to explain to each other what specifically in the sentences led them to make the inferences. Ask students if there are any other inferences that they made while reading. Or have students look at the picture of Curiosity on page 15. Ask them what they can infer from the picture and the information in the caption.

BUILDING VOCABULARY

A. Have students complete Exercise A individually before checking answers in pairs. A person who is described as a *visionary* is an innovative thinker who helps shape the future of society in some way. The noun *prospect* is used as a synonym for *possibility* in the passage. *Extension:* Have students work in pairs to paraphrase the information they read about Captain James Cook in the activity.

B. Have students complete Exercise B individually before checking answers in pairs. Elicit the part of speech for each vocabulary item, and then have students work individually to write definitions. *Extension:* Have students read their definitions to a partner. Their partner must try to guess which target vocabulary item is being defined.

C. Give students a few minutes to discuss the questions in pairs before sharing answers and ideas with the class. Make sure students understand that there are visionaries in every field, not just exploration. *Extension:* Ask students to write a response to one of the questions using as many target vocabulary items as possible.

GETTING MEANING FROM CONTEXT

Ensure that students read the full sentence before choosing the phrase that is closest in meaning. Check answers as a class. Have students write a sentence in an alternative context with each of the four phrases.

CRITICAL THINKING

Applying. Have students work in pairs or small groups to draw up a list of any famous explorers that they know. Give a time limit of three to five minutes. When students have finished, feedback answers as a class, and write students' ideas on the board. *Extension:* Ask students to discuss or write about a time when they explored a new place. How did they feel? What motivated them?

EXPLORE MORE

Ask students to share any background information that they have about Captain Cook, including what they read in the unit. Then have them read the article on the National Geographic website.

WHY WE NEED THE EXPLORERS

LESSON OVERVIEW

Aims:
- Watch and understand a talk about why curiosity-driven science is important.
- Understand key details.
- Understand the main message.

TED Talk Summary: In his TED Talk, physicist Brian Cox explains why public funding for curiosity-driven science is essential. Cox shares his concern about the negative effects that may result from cutting public funding for scientific research. He talks about past scientific discoveries that changed the world. He also talks about the economic impact that space exploration has on the world, including job creation and the invention of technology that changes our lives and moves us forward as humans. An annotated transcript for the edited TED Talk is on pages 71–73 of this Teacher's Guide.

TEACHING NOTES

The paragraphs tell us about Cox's career and his goals. Through his work as a scientist, TV host, and public figure, he is committed to educating others on the importance of public funding for scientific research. Have students work individually to read the paragraphs and answer the questions before checking answers in pairs. *Extension:* Have students work in pairs to go online to find out more about Cox's work at CERN or his job as a TV host. Then have them share what they learned with a pair who researched his other job.

PART 1

PREVIEWING

A. Have students work individually to read the paragraph and answer the questions before checking answers in pairs. Elicit or explain the meaning of *public spending*. Note that a synonym is *public funding*. *Extension:* Have students search online to find out more about public funding for scientific research in their home countries. Then have them share what they learned with the class.

B. Focus students on the picture of Enceladus. Elicit ideas from the class about what exactly the white things coming from the surface are. Write students' ideas on the board.

UNDERSTANDING KEY DETAILS

Have students read the questions first. For question 3, point out that students should choose two answers. Then play the video. Have students check their answers in pairs.

CRITICAL THINKING

Inferring. First, give students a few minutes to think about and write their ideas individually. Note that answers may vary depending on students' own thoughts about the pictures, but for the most part, students should come to the conclusion that both pictures illustrate unexpected findings, or results, of space exploration.

PART 2

PREDICTING

Give students a few minutes to think and write down their ideas. Then have them share their ideas with a partner and brainstorm further possibilities. Tell them to think about how exploration in space has benefited us here on Earth. Then play the video to have students check their answers. *Extension:* Before playing the video, elicit students' ideas. Write them on the board. After students watch, go back to their ideas and discuss them further. Did Cox mention the same points?

UNDERSTANDING KEY DETAILS

Give students a few minutes to put the events in the correct sequence before checking answers in pairs. Elicit answers, writing a timeline on the board of the events. Then ask students to comment on how this example helps support Cox's main message. *Extension:* Have students work in pairs to search online for items made from silicon that are used today. Elicit examples.

UNDERSTANDING THE MAIN MESSAGE

Have students work individually to answer the questions before discussing their answers in pairs. For question 2, remind students of their discussion for **Previewing** of Part 1 of Cox's talk. *Extension:* Elicit some examples of curiosity-based science, in any areas of science: cutting-edge medical research, new kinds of technology, etc.

1. physicist, professor, TV show host; **2.** In each of his professions, Cox champions scientific research.; **3.** If we believe our triumphs and progress are complete, we won't push ourselves to explore and learn further.

PART 1

Previewing

A. By "curiosity-led science," Cox means research that is exploratory, aiming to discover something new and exciting, instead of further working on what we already know; during difficult economic times, funding for curiosity-led science may be cut as governments seek to decrease public spending.

B. Guesses will vary. The actual answer is: ice fountains/water vapor.

Understanding Key Details

1. b; **2.** Scientists believe there is water below the surface of this moon. On our planet, water is synonymous with life.; **3.** b, e

Critical Thinking

Answers will vary. Both photographs show us what we've learned from exploration.

PART 2

Predicting

1. Answers will vary. Possibilities include: employment opportunities, new scientific knowledge, new technology, inspiration given to a new generation to pursue careers in science.

Understanding Key Details

from left to right: 3, 1, 6, 5, 2, 4

Understanding the Main Message

1. a, c; **2.** He means that when scientists explore ideas, this curiosity-led research can lead them to exciting new finds. These scientists are open to experimenting and making new discoveries.

Critical Thinking

Analyzing. 1. b; **2.** Answers will vary.

Reflecting. He explains how in science one discovery leads to another and another, and this chain of discoveries sometimes involve life-altering ones as well. He is also speaking about how some discoveries are made almost by accident while researching something else entirely, which makes all kinds of scientific research even more important.

CRITICAL THINKING

Analyzing. First, give students a few minutes to read the paragraph, answer the first question, and think about and write their ideas individually. Then check answers as a class and elicit a discussion for question 2. *Extension:* Divide the class in half and have them debate whether or not public funding for science is as important as Cox says it is.

Reflecting. Give students a few minutes to think about their answers. If necessary, elicit or explain the meaning of *serendipity*. Make sure students understand that Cox is talking about discoveries that happen by chance or a "happy coincidence." However, note that he is also saying that if these scientists were not driven by curiosity to explore new ideas, they would not have been in the position to encounter this serendipitous moment that led to an important discovery.

EXPLORE MORE

Cox's full TED Talk is just under 17 minutes long. He takes his audience deep into the universe to show what exciting things we are still finding, even from technologically outdated probes.

RESEARCHING AND PRESENTING PRODUCTS

PROJECT OVERVIEW:

Aims:
- Students work in pairs to research a technology developed as a result of space exploration.
- Students present on the history, use, and benefits of the technology.
- The class discusses which of the products are the most useful.

Summary: Students work with a partner to choose a product or technological process that was created as a result of space exploration. Students research the product's connection to space exploration. Pairs present to the class about the technology, and then the class discusses which products are the most useful.

Materials: computer, presentation software, poster board and colored pens

Language Support: Presentation language: *Today I am going to introduce . . . ; Let me first explain . . . ; Let's next talk about . . .*

TEACHING NOTES

PREPARATION

Have students work in pairs. Point out that the main goal of the presentation is to talk about the "unanticipated benefits" of space exploration. Elicit or explain the meaning of this phrase. Ask pairs to look over the list of technologies and discuss which one to focus on. Tell students that they can also choose another technology or product that they know was developed as a result of space exploration. Note the "Language Support" phrases above on the board and review them before students begin the activity.

DURING THE PROJECT

Give students enough time to research their products. Note the two points listed in Activity 2 on page 23 that students should focus on in their research. Remind students that they also need to find a picture or video that shows how the product works. Point out that every presentation should include information about the space program from which the technology originated, some current uses of the technology, and who has benefited most from it. Monitor as pairs plan their presentations, and give assistance or feedback when necessary. Give pairs time to practice their presentations once before presenting to the class.

AFTER THE PROJECT

When pairs present, remind the students listening to take notes and think of questions. After all pairs have presented, ask the class to discuss the different items and technologies. Ask students to share which technologies or products they use the most in their everyday lives. Encourage students to offer examples of how space technology has affected their daily lives. *Extension:* Have students work in pairs or groups to decide what kind of product or technology developed from space exploration will affect our lives next. Have students research technology being developed now for future space missions, and ask them to think about how that technology might be used in our everyday lives. Have each group present their idea to the class.

EXPLORE MORE

Have students go online to learn more about current space exploration. Ask them to consider the benefits of each area of exploration for society as a whole.

SUCCESS AND FAILURE

UNIT OVERVIEW

Reading: Students read about an online mentoring program that connects students and teachers across the world.

TED Talk: Educator Diana Laufenberg argues that schools should shift their focus to experiential learning.

Project: Students research and present on famous individuals who experienced failure before success.

Lesson 2A A SCHOOL IN THE CLOUD

LESSON OVERVIEW

Aims:
- Read and comprehend an article about a new kind of teacher: the Skype Granny.
- Understand main ideas and supporting details.
- Recognize point of view.

Target Vocabulary: constraint, contagious, enthusiasm, facility, guarantee, input, let go of, mentor, prescribe, security

Reading Passage Summary: Students read about an educational program developed by a TED prize winner that allows teachers and students in different countries to have classes together using the online video conferencing program Skype. The teachers are known as Skype Grannies. Students read an interview with a Skype Granny who shares about his experiences teaching children in India from his home in France.

TEACHING NOTES

THINK AND DISCUSS

For question 1, elicit changes in the school experience over the last 100 years. Write a timeline on the board with students' ideas. Note that question 2 relates more to the topic of Lesson B than what students will read about in Lesson A. Elicit students' ideas and opinions, encouraging them to give reasons and examples to support them.

PRE-READING

A. Have students quickly look over the picture and read the caption. Tell them to discuss the questions with a partner. **Extension:** Have students find out more about SOLEs: self-organized learning environments. Ask them to work in pairs to search online and take notes on what they find. Have pairs then share what they learned with another pair.

B. Give students a minute to read the introduction and answer the questions. Have students work individually before checking their answers in pairs. For question 2,

Think and Discuss

1. Answers will vary. Technology has changed schools and education considerably, but areas of curriculum and even classroom setup have also changed.
2. Answers will vary.

Pre-reading

A. Guesses will vary. Actual answer is: The woman is a teacher. She is having a teaching session over Skype with children in India. This type of teacher is called a Skype Granny.

B. 1. The School in the Cloud is a program in which teachers around the world mentor students in India and other countries online.; **2.** Answers will vary. Advantages may include students and teachers both getting a more diverse experience, students getting teachers who are experts in certain fields, retired teachers having a chance to continue to contribute to a society, etc. Disadvantages may include technological problems, communication problems, etc.

C. b, c, e

Getting the Main Ideas

A. a. 4; **b.** 6; **c.** 1; **d.** 3; **e.** 2; **f.** 5

B. 1. a; **2.** c; **3.** b; **4.** a; **5.** c; **6.** a

Finding Supporting Details

Answers may vary somewhat.; **1.** he watched a TV show about it; **2.** by talking about things that happened during the week; photos, video, or written material; to talk about the material and give input; **3.** sound, video, or the Internet connection; **4.** when students made him get-well cards; **5.** enthusiasm for the subject; the ability to work within the constraints of the existing system; **6.** children take more charge of their learning

Recognizing Point of View

1. He is critical of the current system. He thinks schools are focusing too much on national exam scores. Parts of his answer to question 5 should be underlined by students. Possibilities include: "we moved to a very prescribed curriculum with little or no time to drift sideways . . . ," " . . . school's examination results became the most important thing . . ."

B. Answers will vary. Possibilities include:

Swancott's view of current approaches to education: curriculum is not flexible enough, schools are too focused on national examination results, learning is too controlled by teacher and school, etc.

Swancott's ideas for better approach to teaching: teacher acts as facilitator, use technology to create new learning opportunities, let children take charge of their learning, let go of control over learning experience of students, etc.

Building Vocabulary

A. 1. constraints; **2.** input; **3.** let go of; **4.** enthusiastic; **5.** facilities

B. 1. input; **2.** constraints; **3.** facilities; **4.** guarantee; **5.** enthusiastic

C. 1–3. Answers will vary.

Getting Meaning from Context

1. a; **2.** b; **3.** b; **4.** b

Critical Thinking

1. He describes the children as very enthusiastic about the opportunity to learn from him, as well as appreciative. He believes he is creating a teaching environment that allows the students to lead their learning, which benefits them.

2. Answers will vary.

---

elicit a class discussion about online learning environments. *Extension:* Ask students to offer ideas about why the program is called the School in the Cloud.

C. Explain that the passage is an interview with a Skype Granny. Have students work individually to look at the interview questions and complete the activity before checking answers in pairs.

DEVELOPING READING SKILLS

GETTING THE MAIN IDEAS

A. Have students read the entire passage, either silently or while listening to the narrated passage on the audio. Have them work individually to complete the activity. For Exercise A, encourage students to focus on the interview questions that often introduce the main ideas.

B. Have students work individually before checking answers in pairs.

FINDING SUPPORTING DETAILS

Have students work individually or in pairs to complete the outline. Elicit answers and write the outline on the board in the form of a concept map. Note that students' wording may vary, but the general idea should be the same for each supporting detail.

RECOGNIZING POINT OF VIEW

A. Note that students should focus on Swancott's answer to question 5; however, let students find this out on their own. Have students work in pairs or individually to answer the questions before checking answers in class. Elicit what parts of the passage were underlined and why.

B. Have students complete the chart in pairs before checking answers as a class. Note that students should list three ideas for each category. Answers may vary depending on which points students decide to pick up. *Extension:* Ask students to comment on whether they agree or not with Swancott's ideas about a better approach to teaching.

BUILDING VOCABULARY

A. Have students work individually to complete the sentences before checking answers in pairs. The word *input* in this case describes a contribution on the part of the students, but it can also refer to what the teacher brings to the class, as in Exercise B. *Input* is often used to talk about what is put into a system of some sort; however, when a person has *input* in a situation, they have a say and a role in what is happening.

B. Have students work individually before checking answers as a class. *Extension:* Ask students to summarize what they learned about SOLEs in the paragraph.

C. Have students discuss answers in pairs. A *mentor* is someone with experience in a certain area who tries to help someone with less experience grow and succeed at something.

GETTING MEANING FROM CONTEXT

Have students work individually to complete the activity. Encourage them to go back to the reading passage to look at the phrases being used in context. Check answers as a class. *Extension:* Have students write new sentences using the phrases in the activity.

CRITICAL THINKING

1. Evaluating. If necessary, elicit or explain the meaning of the expression "make a difference." Give students time to go back to the passage to find examples that Swancott gives of how he feels he is positively impacting the students. Note that he also talks about how they've positively impacted him. *Extension:* Have students also find evidence about how the students in India are making a difference in Swancott's life.

2. Personalizing. Have students share their ideas in pairs. Then choose one question to elicit a class discussion about, encouraging students to give reasons and examples to support their opinions and ideas.

EXPLORE MORE

The School in the Cloud is also being used in various countries around the world. Some countries mentioned on the program's website include Greenland, Cambodia, and Mexico, for example. Encourage students to also search for the Granny Cloud online, a blog that supports Skype Grannies.

HOW TO LEARN? FROM MISTAKES

LESSON OVERVIEW

Aims:

- Watch and understand a talk about the value of letting students fail.
- Integrate information.
- Analyze an argument.
- Recognize tone.

TED Talk Summary: In her TED Talk, educator Diana Laufenberg argues that teachers need to let students fail more. She believes that experiential learning is the most effective kind for students, as it empowers the learners and teaches them resilience as failure becomes a valuable part of their learning process. An annotated transcript for the edited TED Talk is on pages 74–75 of this Teacher's Guide.

TEACHING NOTES

The paragraph introduces the ideas of Diana Laufenberg by describing her commitment to experiential learning and belief that failure and making mistakes helps students grow and makes them better learners. Have students work individually to read the paragraphs and answer the questions. Ask them to check in pairs before eliciting a class discussion about experiential learning.

PART 1

PREVIEWING

Have students work individually to read the paragraph. If necessary, elicit the meaning of "that's where the information lived." Have students discuss their answers to the question in pairs or elicit a class discussion. Ask students to share examples of their grandparents' educational experience versus their own. Ask them for both similarities and differences. *Extension:* Have students also compare their parents' educational experience with their own.

GETTING THE MAIN IDEAS

A. Give students 30 seconds to look over the chart in Exercise A. Then play the video. Tell students to work individually to complete the chart before checking answers in pairs.

B. Have pairs discuss their ideas about why the encyclopedia was significant. *Extension:* Tell students to name all the sources of information that they now have available in their homes. Ask them which one they use the most.

INTEGRATING INFORMATION

A. Have students work individually to complete the activity before checking answers in pairs. Point out that students should choose two answers. *Extension:* Ask students to use what they've learned so far in the lesson to talk about Laufenberg's views on how to teach.

B. Have students work individually to write down their ideas before discussing in pairs. Note that students should understand that Laufenberg is saying that because information is so readily accessible these days, the role of school has to change. School is no longer where students come to get information, and schools have to change their approaches to teaching and education as a result.

CRITICAL THINKING

Predicting. Give students a few minutes to discuss their ideas with a partner. Tell them to think about what makes them motivated to come to school. Elicit a class discussion to hear students' ideas. Ask students to support their ideas with examples from their personal experiences as students.

PART 2

ANALYZING AN ARGUMENT

A. Have students work individually to read the excerpt. If necessary, elicit or explain the meaning of *infographic* and *man-made disaster*. Then ask students to explain the meaning of the phrase "Go figure it out." Have students look over the questions. Then play the video. Have students work individually to write answers before checking answers as a class. For question 3, make sure students understand that Laufenberg's students did not make effective infographics for various reasons. The example she gives shows us one with good graphics but an ineffective presentation of information. *Extension:* Ask students to share with a partner a time at school when they failed, and what they learned from the experience.

1. Answers will vary. Experiential learning involves learning through doing, such as internships and group or independent projects. This learning style is especially effective when it involves time to reflect on the experience.; **2.** Answers will vary. Such experiences provide both a range of learning opportunities as well as a comfortable environment (back in the classroom) to evaluate and reflect.; **3.** *Resilience* involves being able to come back from a failure or difficult situation and do well again. Students with resilience will be more able to learn from mistakes and use those lessons to go on to have success.

PART 1

Previewing

Answers will vary. For many students, technology will be a major difference.

Getting the Main Ideas

A. Laufenberg's grandmother and father: information is only at school, information comes from teacher to student; **Laufenberg:** had encyclopedias at home

B. The encyclopedia set at home made information close by and easily accessible.

Integrating Information

A. 2, 3

B. Her goals involved investigating what a school needs to be like to motivate students to come in an age when school is no longer the primary place where students get information.

Critical Thinking

Answers will vary. Laufenberg is focused on lessons that are led by students, so they learn how to effectively make use of all the information around them.

PART 2

Analyzing an Argument

A. 1. No. It was their first time making infographics and they were uncomfortable with the task.; **2.** She wanted them to learn how to do it on their own, including thinking about what goes into a successful infographic.; **3.** Most students did not make effective infographics.; **4.** Next time they will improve their performances because they are learning from their mistakes.

B. Answers will vary. Because students evaluated and talked about what wasn't successful in the infographics, they were able to learn how to improve future ones.

Recognizing Tone and Attitude

A. 2

B. 1. critical; **2.** Possibilities include: we're missing the mark, does not value, we won't get there, it's time to do better; **3.** experiential learning, empowering students, embracing failure

Critical Thinking

1. Answers will vary. Note that students should answer the questions: *What do you think makes a good teacher? What do you think is the future of learning?*; **2.** Laufenberg believes in teachers and ways of teaching with a focus on experiential learning, student-led learning, and allowing students to fail.; **3.** Both Swancott and Laufenberg agree that children should lead the learning process. And they both agree that the current educational system needs to be fixed, although Swancott is talking about the British educational system and Laufenberg about the American one.

B. Give students a minute to think about their answers before discussing in pairs.

RECOGNIZING TONE AND ATTITUDE

A. Have students work individually before checking answers in pairs. Explain that Laufenberg's tone is also very apparent when listening to her voice. *Extension:* Play the video again to have students listen for how her intonation changes when she is emphasizing a point.

B. Have students work in pairs or small groups. Let them do Exercise B as a student-led activity. Don't give them any instruction. After they discuss, check answers as a class. Then elicit a class discussion to hear whether students agree with Laufenberg's ideas or not. *Extension:* Ask students to write or talk about the current educational policies in their home countries and what kind of learning is most encouraged.

CRITICAL THINKING

Synthesizing. If necessary, play Part 2 of the video again. Give students time to go back to Lesson A to review Swancott's opinions. If necessary, have students answer the questions from the video and the reading first, and then go back to question 1 to talk about their own opinions. For question 1, elicit a class discussion to hear students' thoughts and ideas.

EXPLORE MORE

Laufenberg's full TED Talk is under nine minutes. Encourage students to identify examples that Laufenberg gives to further support her main idea.

 Project

WRITING A PROFILE ABOUT SOMEONE WHO OVERCAME FAILURE

PROJECT OVERVIEW:

Aims:

- Students write a profile of a famous person who succeeded after a major failure.
- Students research and tell the story of how failure helped this person.
- Students present their profiles with supporting visuals to the class.

Summary: Students research a successful person who learned from failures. Students first write a profile about the individual and then give a presentation to their classmates.

Materials: computer, presentation software and/or poster board, pens

Language Support: Describing final results: *In the end, . . . ; Eventually, . . . ; Ultimately, . . . ; At the end of the day, . . .*

TEACHING NOTES

PREPARATION

Have students work individually or in pairs. Explain that they are going to research and write about a famous person who experienced failure before success. Tell them that they will present this profile to the class along with visual aids to accompany the talk. Give students time to look over the names on the list and do some light research to learn more about them. Note the "Language Support" phrases above on the board and review them before students begin the activity.

DURING THE PROJECT

As much as possible, make this project an experiential learning exercise for students. Give them a lot of freedom to lead the creation of their reports and presentations. Encourage them to use the questions in part B on page 39 to guide their research. Give them enough time to search online and learn the necessary details about their individuals, and write the profiles. Have students also search online for pictures and visuals to accompany their talks. Tell them to think about how to make their presentations both informative and entertaining.

AFTER THE PROJECT

After all students have presented, elicit a class discussion. Who had the most spectacular failure? Who learned the most valuable lesson? *Extension:* As each student presents, tell the listeners to pay close attention and to think about both positives and negatives about the presentation. When all students have presented, have a class discussion about whether the presentations were failures or successes. Ask students to reflect on and talk about what they might do differently next time.

POWER SHIFTS

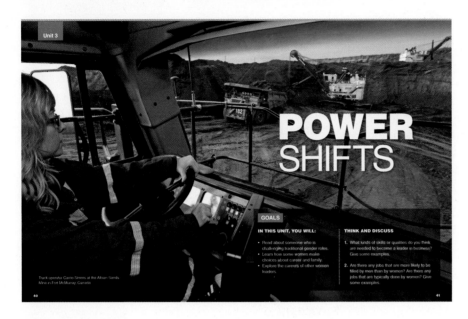

UNIT OVERVIEW

Reading: Students read about a young woman in India who has opened a door for other women to work in a male-dominated profession.

TED Talk: Sheryl Sandberg talks about why there aren't as many women as men at the tops of companies and suggests how this can be changed.

Project: Students research and make a presentation about a woman who's had great success in her profession.

 **Lesson 3A** ## DRIVING CHANGE

LESSON OVERVIEW

Aims:
- Read and comprehend an article about a young woman's idea to provide a new job opportunity for women living in the slums of Delhi.
- Understand key details.
- Interpret statistics.
- Recognize reference markers.

Target Vocabulary: aspire, collaboration, donate, endorse, found, fulfill, mirror, stereotype, take on, volunteer

Reading Passage Summary: Students read about a young woman in India who at age 17 started a rickshaw-driving program for women in the slums of Delhi. Rickshaw driving is a job traditionally done only by males in India, so the introduction of female workers to this field has opened new chances for poor women to find economic independence and empowerment.

TEACHING NOTES

THINK AND DISCUSS

The unit explores societal attitudes toward women and work, especially in regards to positions of power and leadership. Note that students will likely have varying impressions and opinions about working women depending on their home countries and cultures. As much as possible, let this be a student-led learning experience in which students explore and challenge beliefs and stereotypes that they each have about women in the workforce. Both of the **Think and Discuss** questions help students explore their own thoughts on the topic. For question 1, have students work in pairs to brainstorm a list of leadership qualities. Then elicit a class discussion and write the qualities on the board. *Extension:* Have students work individually to write an essay about what the working environment is like for women in their home countries. Do women work outside the home? What kinds of jobs do they have? What kinds of salaries are typical? Do women continue to work after marriage?

Think and Discuss

1. Answers will vary. Possibilities include: diplomacy, decision-making skills, team-building skills, authority.; 2. Answers will vary.

Pre-reading

A. 1–3. Answers will vary. Possibilities include: 1. It has been male-dominated because rickshaw driving takes a lot of physical strength.; 2. Opening up rickshaw driving to women will help create many new jobs for women, especially those without a formal education. It is also a flexible job timewise, so women can schedule it around home duties as well.; 3. One necessary step will be finding a way that women can easily power a rickshaw.

B. 1. Less than 30 percent; 2. The female labor force in India is one of the smallest in the world, in relation to population size.

C. Students should understand that female rickshaw drivers are being introduced to the workforce.

Getting the Main Ideas

5, 4, 2

Understanding Key Details

Counterclockwise from top left: 16/17, Avani Singh, economic, single, hope, women, environmentally friendly

Interpreting Statistics

1. 50 percent; 2. stayed the same (16 percent); 3. Possibilities include: Vietnam, Cambodia, Nepal, Mozambique, Rwanda, Tanzania.; 4. smallest gap: Canada, Vietnam, Cambodia, Nepal, Mozambique, Rwanda, Tanzania; biggest gap: Jordan, Pakistan, India, Turkey, Mexico; 5. Answers will vary. Possibilities include: cultural and societal attitudes toward women in the workforce.

Recognizing Reference Markers

Paragraph 1. "these fields" = engineering and technology; **Paragraph 2.** "this figure" = 50 percent of all women worldwide participate in the workforce; "This last figure" = 16 percent of working women work in industry or technology; **Paragraph 4.** "This city of 17 million" = New Delhi/Delhi; "these areas of poverty" = slums; **Paragraph 6.** "this initiative" = Ummeed ki Rickshaw/Singh's program to train female rickshaw drivers; **Paragraph 7.** "the idea" = female rickshaw drivers; **Paragraph 8.** "a city" = Delhi/New Delhi

Building Vocabulary

A. 1. stereotype; 2. endorsed; 3. collaborated; 4. donated; 5. volunteers

B. 1. is similar to; 2. established; 3. hope; 4. perform; 5. accept

C. Answers will vary.

Getting Meaning from Context

1. b; 2. f; 3. c; 4. g; 5. d

Critical Thinking

1. The "hard facts" refer to statistics about women in the workforce, namely that 50 percent of women in the workforce are employed in service-level jobs, instead of corporate jobs that lead to leadership positions and better salaries.; 2. There is still only a small proportion of women worldwide who hold jobs outside agriculture or service industries.

PRE-READING

A. Give students a minute or so to think about and write their answers before discussing with a partner. Tell them to look only at the photo on pages 42 and 43 when making their predictions.

B. Give students less than a minute to scan the graph and answer the questions. Have them check answers in pairs. *Extension:* Ask partners to talk about women in the workforce in their home countries.

C. Give students a few minutes to skim the article and answer the question. Have them discuss in pairs.

Students should understand that Singh has started a program that employs women as rickshaw drivers, which has the potential to create a major shift in this otherwise male-dominated job field.

DEVELOPING READING SKILLS

GETTING THE MAIN IDEAS

Have students read the entire passage, either silently or while listening to the narrated passage on the audio. Have them work individually to complete the activity before checking answers in pairs. *Extension:* Ask partners to discuss why rickshaw driving might be an especially good field for women to work in. Encourage them to think about work-life balance.

UNDERSTANDING KEY DETAILS

Note that students should fill out the map in a counter-clockwise direction, starting with the rectangle in the top left, to get details in the order that they appear in the passage. Have students work individually to complete the activity before checking answers in pairs. *Extension:* Ask students to put the key details together to create a summary of the story. Tell them to paraphrase the information in their own words.

INTERPRETING STATISTICS

Have students read the questions first in order to scan for information more effectively. Give students a few minutes to find all the information before checking answers in pairs. Note that for questions 3 and 4, there are multiple answer choices. Give students a few minutes to reread the information in the sidebar. For question 5, elicit a class discussion. Encourage students to share what the workforce looks like in their own countries. *Extension:* If students' countries are not listed in the graph, ask them to go online and find out the statistics for their home countries. Ask students if the statistic surprised them or not.

RECOGNIZING REFERENCE MARKERS

Explain that reference markers help add variety to what a writer is saying, so the same subject/object or pronoun does not need to be repeated over and over again. In this case, the writer is using general categories and words, instead of pronouns or names, to refer back to information already mentioned. Give students enough time to go back to the passage to find each of the references and identify the topic. Have them work individually before checking answers as a class. Elicit where in the passage students found the original idea for each answer.

BUILDING VOCABULARY

A. Have students complete Exercise A individually. Point out that students may need to change the part of speech. Have students check answers in pairs. The verb *endorse* is used in cases when something is approved of in a public forum. The subject doing the endorsing usually has influence, such as a government, a well-known organization, institution, politician, celebrity, etc.

B. Have students complete Exercise B individually before checking answers as a class. When you "take on" something, you accept it as your responsibility and commit to it. *Extension:* Have students write new sentences, or a paragraph, about women in the workforce for each of the vocabulary items in Exercises A and B.

C. Give students a minute to think about their answers before discussing in pairs. Ask students to share what they discussed for question 2. Encourage a discussion about stereotypes about women. Elicit students' opinions and ideas on the topic.

GETTING MEANING FROM CONTEXT

Have students work individually or in pairs to complete the activity before checking answers as a class. Elicit new sentences for each of the expressions. Note that two definitions are not needed. *Extension:* Have students work in pairs to discuss the following question: Do you think it's harder for women to strike a balance between home life and work life than it is for men? Why?

CRITICAL THINKING

Interpreting. If necessary, elicit or explain the meaning and use of "hard facts." Make sure students understand that it refers to reliable information. Note that the term is often joined with the adjective *cold* to emphasize that the information is impartial and true: the cold, hard facts. Give students a minute to think about and write their answers in pairs. Then elicit a class discussion to have students share their thoughts.

EXPLORE MORE

Cequin is the Centre for Equity and Inclusion in India, the organization that supported Singh's initiative by putting out a call for volunteers for her program. It is a non-profit that attempts to help groups in India who are generally not empowered in society, especially women and girls.

WHY WE HAVE TOO FEW WOMEN LEADERS

LESSON OVERVIEW

Aims:
- Watch and understand a talk about why there are so few women leaders.
- Understand main ideas and key details.
- Understand purpose.

TED Talk Summary: In her TED Talk, business executive Sheryl Sandberg talks about why she thinks there are so few women in leadership positions. Then she offers advice for women who choose to continue their careers as they raise families. She talks about a difference in self-confidence between men and women, and how it affects women's choices at work. She suggests that women must see themselves as important decision makers and worthy of being a part of meetings and discussions in order to find more success in business. An annotated transcript for the edited TED Talk is on pages 76–78 of this Teacher's Guide.

TEACHING NOTES

The paragraph introduces Sheryl Sandberg and her concerns about the lack of women in senior positions. Use the content and questions to provide students with background for what they will hear in the video. Encourage them to also rely on what they learned in Lesson A. Have students work individually to answer the questions before checking answers as a class. For question 3, elicit a class discussion or have students work alone to further develop their ideas.

PART 1

PREVIEWING AND PREDICTING

A. Give students a few minutes to work individually to read the paragraphs and answer the questions. Check answers as a class. For question 2, elicit a class discussion. Note that students have already encountered some similar global statistics in the reading passage in Lesson A.

B. Have students work in pairs. Ask them to discuss their ideas and answers to the questions based on what they read in the paragraphs in Exercise A and any background information they already have on the topic. For question 1, elicit the meaning of the expression "in the wrong direction." For question 2, ask pairs to share with the class the problem that they

think Sandberg is going to talk about. Encourage students to talk about any connection between their answers to question 1 and question 2. Then play the video to have students check their answers.

GETTING THE MAIN IDEAS

Have students work individually to answer the question before checking answers as a class. Ask students how the statistic that Sandberg shares (that only one-third of married female managers have children as opposed to two-thirds of men) illustrates this problem.

PART 2

PREVIEWING

Note that the excerpts on page 53 are not from the edited video that students will watch, but instead from the full-length talk. Part 1 ended with Sandberg making three suggestions, but only one of them will be talked about in detail in Part 2 of the talk. The excerpts here explain the other two for students. Have students work individually to answer the questions before checking answers as a class.

UNDERSTANDING MAIN IDEAS

Play the video. Have students work individually to answer the questions before checking answers in pairs. *Extension:* Ask students to share with a partner a time when they did or didn't "sit at the table."

UNDERSTANDING KEY DETAILS

A. Have students work individually to complete the Venn diagram. Check answers as a class after Exercise B.

B. Give students a minute to think about their ideas before discussing with a partner. Then check answers as a class to Exercises A and B, eliciting a discussion about stereotypes of successful women in business. *Extension:* Ask students to comment on whether or not they agree that successful women are seen as less likeable than successful men.

UNDERSTANDING PURPOSE

Explain to students that during presentations, speakers often tell anecdotes to build upon the point they are making. Have students discuss their answers to the questions in pairs.

1. She was originally an economist for the World Bank, and then she worked for Google, managing online sales operations.; 2. She is concerned that women who choose to remain in the workforce aren't confident and assertive, and they don't end up in leadership positions as a result. She is also concerned about negative attitudes toward ambitious female employees.; 3. Answers will vary.

PART 1

Previewing and Predicting

A. 1. She is focusing on jobs at the top of companies and industries, such as CEOs, COOs, CFOs, etc.; 2. Answers will vary.

B. 1–2. Guesses will vary. Actual answers are: 1. According to Sandberg, part of the problem comes from the difficulty of balancing work and family. Women are often not as assertive in their careers because they are also considering the time and energy that will be needed to take care of their families.; 2. In the next part of her talk, Sandberg speaks about negative attitudes in the corporate world toward successful and assertive women, whereas men with similar career paths are praised and considered likeable.

Getting the Main Ideas

The following should be checked: 2

PART 2

Previewing

1. Sandberg means that women shouldn't stop being assertive and seeking promotions because they are thinking ahead to a time in the future when they may want to have a family. Changing your career decisions based on family obligations before you even have family obligations ultimately affects your chances of getting into a top position in your company.; 2. Sandberg is referring to a marital partner here. She is saying that the work that each spouse does at home has to be equal in order for the female partner to succeed at work. Otherwise, she is too overwhelmed by the many responsibilities she has outside of work, which then also affects her career choices.

Understanding Main Ideas

1. a, b; 2. a

Understanding Key Details

A. Heidi: d, e

Howard: b, c

Both: a

B. The "Heidi story" illustrates that women with equal capabilities to men will likely have a harder time getting a promotion. Successful women are stereotyped as less likeable than successful men, which is why women will have to be their own best supporter in their careers, including not being afraid to ask for more money, as promotions and raises will not come as easily to them as to their male colleagues.

Understanding Purpose

1. She noticed that even though Sandberg said that she wouldn't take any more questions, the men kept their hands raised in case there was a chance. And Sandberg did end up answering more questions, all from men.; 2. That she and her fellow female colleagues weren't assertive enough, and too quick to put their hands down.; 3. Sandberg is illustrating that even she is capable of demonstrating behavior influenced by mistaken attitudes that favor men at work.

Critical Thinking

1–2. Answers will vary.

CRITICAL THINKING

1. Evaluating. Give students time to think individually before discussing in pairs. Tell students to give reasons and examples to support their opinions.

2. Reflecting. Have students discuss in pairs. Tell them to include as many details as possible in their anecdotes. Ask them to talk about how the choice affected the person's life after, in both positive and negative ways.

EXPLORE MORE

Have students watch Sandberg's full TED Talk to learn more about the two other ways that Sandberg suggests women can stay in the workforce.

RESEARCHING WOMEN WITH SUCCESSFUL CAREERS

PROJECT OVERVIEW:

Aims:
- Students research and gather information about a woman at the top of her profession.
- Students consider the issues they read and thought about in the unit while gathering information about the individual.
- Students present their findings to the class.

Summary: Students give a brief presentation about a famous woman who has reached the top of her industry or profession. Students use what they learned in the unit to support their research and presentation content. The class discusses each report and talks about why and how each woman came to be successful.

Materials: access to the Internet, presentation software or poster board and pens

Language Support: Describing work responsibilities: *She's responsible for . . . ; She's in charge of . . . ; She's the head of . . . ; Her work involves . . . ; She's involved in . . .*

TEACHING NOTES

PREPARATION

Give pairs time to look over the list and choose an individual. Tell them they can also choose another famous female who is at the top of her profession or industry. Monitor students' choices to make sure that a variety of individuals are represented overall. Explain that students should use the prompts on page 55 to guide their research. Ask them to think about the kinds of sacrifices the woman has had to make on the road to success. Ask them to pay particular attention to balancing work and family life. Note the "Language Support" phrases on the board and review them before students begin the activity.

DURING THE PROJECT

Monitor as students prepare their presentations. Remind them that the presentation should be brief, so they should think carefully about what information is most important to include. Give pairs a few minutes to practice their presentations before giving them to the class. While pairs are presenting, remind other students to listen carefully and take notes. Encourage students to think of questions to ask each other.

AFTER THE PROJECT

Ask the class to talk about what they learned from each other and share what they want to know more about. Give students time to tell even more about the individuals they researched if there was content they weren't able to include in the two minutes of the presentation. ***Extension:*** Elicit a class discussion by asking students to talk about how their views about women in the workforce have changed during the unit.

EXPLORE MORE

For a TED speaker who agrees with Sandberg but at the same time also offers another point of view, have students listen to Anne-Marie Slaughter's talk "Can we 'have it all'?"

CREATIVE SPARKS

UNIT OVERVIEW

Reading: Students read theories about how and why young people's creativity has changed in the last 20 years.

TED Talk: Filmmaker J.J. Abrams talks about the power of mystery in films and why anyone can make movies today.

Project: Students plan to tell a story using the technology available to them.

Lesson 4A   SPARKING WONDER AND POSSIBILITY

LESSON OVERVIEW

Aims:
- Read and comprehend an article about the decline of creative writing skills among younger generations.
- Understand a study.
- Analyze literary excerpts.

Target Vocabulary: analyze, dimension, distinct, genre, highlight, identical, obviously, option, proficiency, societal

Reading Passage Summary: Students read about a study that evaluates the creativity of adolescents today who have grown up using technology and social networks on a daily basis. The study concludes that while visual proficiency has improved, there is a decline in creativity and skills in the area of writing. Young people prefer more narrative realism, such as writing about what is really happening in their lives at the moment. The study points to both the avid use of digital technology among youths, as well as the focus at schools on standardized testing, as being at fault for the decline in interest in writing fiction. The author suggests that more exposure to creative literature will help solve this problem.

TEACHING NOTES

THINK AND DISCUSS

This unit focuses on creativity and how technology is changing the kinds of stories we are telling. Lesson A looks at fiction writing, while Lesson B focuses on filmmaking. Use the **Think and Discuss** questions to explore the kinds of stories and genres that students prefer, and to ask why they favor one over another. *Star Trek* was an American science fiction TV show that first aired in 1966 and later became a movie franchise as well. *Star Trek* combines both science fiction and action. The Lesson B TED Talk speaker directed the most recent *Star Trek* films. ***Extension:*** Have students work in pairs to tell each other about the last movie they saw and what kind of stories they like.

Think and Discuss

1. *Star Trek* is science fiction and an action-adventure. Students' answers regarding the popularity of movies like this will vary.; **2.** Answers will vary.

Pre-reading

A. 1–2. Guesses will vary. Actual answers are: **1.** The app generation is young people who have grown up using tablet computers and smartphones.; **2.** Narrative realism refers to nonfiction writing that is based on personal stories and real-life experiences. Many young people have become accustomed to this style of writing through their use of social media.

B. 1. Both book covers show an element of fantasy, mystery, and perhaps even science fiction.; **2.** Both books are fiction, and both seem to involve mystery and imagination.; **3.** Answers will vary.

Getting the Main Ideas

1. c; **2.** a

Understanding a Study

Answers in order from top to bottom: *Creativity Research Journal*; Harvard Graduate School and University of Washington; to find out how creative writing and art-making by adolescents have changed over the last 20 years; 354 visual artworks and 50 fiction stories; 1990–1995 and 2006–2011; visual proficiency; creativity and technical skill in writing; The increase in digital technology and the rise in standardized testing have contributed to a decline in creativity and imagination in writing.

Critical Thinking

Answers will vary. Kim suggests that what students read and the manner in which they learn and study are affecting their sense of creativity and imagination. What's being inferred is that online and digital content lends itself more to narrative realism than to fiction. Another possible interpretation is that the focus and ways of expressing creativity are changing but not the creativity or imagination itself. Young people may simply be responding to an overall societal trend toward narrative realism now, and not pioneering this trend as suggested by Kim.

Analyzing Literary Excerpts

A. 1. c; **2.** Clues include: The walls were blank and two-dimensional; the walls began to purr and recede into crystalline distance.

B. Answers will vary. Possibilities include: **1.** They are 10 years old and like to use their imaginations.; **2.** They are at home with a babysitter, lying in their bed, imagining being dead.; **3.** Answers will vary. It is likely that the girls will have some kind of fantasy experience of being in a coffin or perhaps feeling what it's like to be dead.

Building Vocabulary

A. 1. distinct; **2.** identical; **3.** proficiency; **4.** highlight; **5.** dimensions

B. 1. options; **2.** analyzing; **3.** Obviously; **4.** societal; **5.** genre

C. 1–2. Answers will vary.

Getting Meaning from Context

A. 1. b; **2.** c; **3.** a

B. Answers will vary. Possibilities include: expose them to various forms of art, encourage them to think and discuss their ideas, have them spend time in nature, etc.

Critical Thinking

Answers will vary.

PRE-READING

A. Give students a few minutes to read the introduction on page 58. Ask them to work individually to write their answers before discussing in pairs. Make sure students understand that an app is computer software that usually is designed for one specific purpose and is used on a smartphone or tablet computer. Apps play a major role in social media and the way that young people interact with written content online. Note that narrative realism here is being contrasted to fantasy and science fiction.

B. Point out that students should answer the questions based only on the book covers. Have students work individually to complete the activity before discussing answers in pairs. Explain that there are no correct answers. ***Extension:*** Have students work in pairs to tell each other about the last book they read and why they chose that book.

DEVELOPING READING SKILLS

GETTING THE MAIN IDEAS

Have students read the entire passage, either silently or while listening to the narrated passage on the audio. Have them work individually to answer the questions before checking answers in pairs. *Extension:* Ask students to discuss whether or not they agree with the conclusion of the research. Have them discuss in pairs first before eliciting a class discussion. Note that it can be argued that fantasy and science fiction in the young-adult fiction genre especially have been on the rise in the last 20 years, taking into consideration the huge success of series like *Harry Potter* and *The Hunger Games*.

UNDERSTANDING A STUDY

Elicit or explain the meaning of "a study." Make sure students understand that the noun refers to a detailed investigation and research into a specific topic. An official research study, like the one discussed in the passage, is usually sponsored by an institution and, when finished, its results are published. Have students work individually or in pairs to complete the information. Check answers as a class. Note that students may paraphrase their answers slightly differently. *Extension:* Ask students to comment on the overall study. Do they think it was accurate and big enough to support the theories that came out of it? What other ways could students' creativity be looked at?

CRITICAL THINKING

Interpreting. Give students time to think about their answers before discussing in pairs. Note that students should first discuss if they think digital technology and standardized testing are to blame for the decline in creativity in relation to writing. Then ask them to think more critically about Kim's interpretations and suggest other possibilities that might also be contributing to a decline in creative writing. *Extension:* Have students write a short science fiction or fantasy story. Then have them share with a partner about their process of writing. Did they struggle to be creative in their writing?

ANALYZING LITERARY EXCERPTS

Explain that students are going to read an excerpt from two different fiction stories with the goal of recognizing basic components and ideas from each story. Students are first asked to make inferences about what is happening in each story and what is going to happen. Note that students should be able to make educated guesses based on the excerpts.

A. and B. Have students work individually or in pairs to read through the excerpts for both Exercise A and B. Allow them to use a dictionary if necessary. Have students complete both activities. Then have them discuss their answers in pairs before checking as a class. For Exercise B, students' answers are likely to vary somewhat. Ensure that any inferences or predictions made are fully justified. *Extension:* Tell students to choose one of the stories and go online to find a longer excerpt to read. Then have students work in pairs to explain more about the story to a partner. Ask them to also share their opinions about the writing style and storyline.

BUILDING VOCABULARY

A. Have students complete Exercise A individually before checking answers as a class. Students may be familiar with the verb *highlight* in regards to marking a text. Point out that when we verbally highlight something, we are essentially doing the same thing—bringing specific attention to it.

B. Have students complete Exercise B individually before checking answers in pairs. The term *genre* is used in art, music, and literature, to name or identify a category. *Extension:* Have students share a movie or story they know that would be considered part of the dystopian genre. Elicit a class discussion to hear students' opinions about this genre.

C. Have students work in pairs to discuss the questions.

GETTING MEANING FROM CONTEXT

A. Have students work individually or in pairs to complete the activity before checking answers as a class. Elicit new sentences for each of the expressions.

B. Give students a few minutes to make a mind map of their ideas. Point out that the author of the reading passage believes that fantasy and science fiction stories can help spark creativity. However, there are actually many different ways to do this. Explain that students don't need to be limited to ideas related to reading. Elicit ideas, encouraging a class brainstorm. Write a mind map on the board.

CRITICAL THINKING

Personalizing. Give students a minute to think about their answers and book recommendations before having them discuss in pairs. If necessary, allow them to go online to find out more about McClure's book recommendations. Ask students to give a summary of their recommendations to their partners.

EXPLORE MORE

Note that Laura McClure's blog article on TED.com is titled "A Science Fiction and Fantasy Reading List for Teen Creativity." Students will find it more quickly by searching by the title instead of the author's name.

Lesson 4B THE MYSTERY BOX

LESSON OVERVIEW

Aims:

- Watch and understand a talk about mystery in storytelling and the role new technology can play in this.
- Understand key details.
- Analyze problems and solutions.

TED Talk Summary: In his TED Talk, film and TV director J.J. Abrams talks about what has inspired him to tell stories that combine mystery with action. Abrams talks about his influences as a young boy and in the process discusses how the element of mystery has been an important one in all of his work. In particular, he talks about his grandfather and a gift that his grandfather gave him. He then goes on to talk about the role of technology in creating mystery in films, and how today's technology makes filmmaking more accessible to anyone with the creative spark to try it. An annotated transcript for the edited TED Talk is on pages 79–81 of this Teacher's Guide.

TEACHING NOTES

The paragraph and questions introduce J.J. Abrams further. While students might not be familiar with Abrams, they may know some of the shows or movies he has directed, including *Alias, Lost, Mission: Impossible III, Star Trek Into Darkness, Star Wars: Episode VII*. A relatively young director, Abrams is known for using technology to create shocking yet realistic action scenes. Have students work individually to read the paragraph and answer the question. Check answers as a class, eliciting any background knowledge that students have about Abrams or his films. *Extension:* Have students work in pairs to find out about one of Abrams's TV shows or movies. Ask them to search online, take notes, and then introduce some information about the show or movie to another pair.

PART 1

PREDICTING

Have students work in pairs to share their ideas about what is in the box and where it came from. Have students look at the photo on page 67. Explain that Abrams refers to it as a "mystery magic box." Ask pairs to share their predictions with the class. Then play the video.

UNDERSTANDING KEY DETAILS

Give students two minutes to work individually to read the excerpt and answer the questions. Check answers as a class, asking students to paraphrase Abrams's story about the magic box. *Extension:* Have students write about something from their childhood that still has important meaning in their life now. Tell them to describe the item and its meaning.

CRITICAL THINKING

Inferring. Give students a few minutes to think about their ideas before having a class discussion. Then ask each student to share whether they would have opened the box or not, and why.

PART 2

PREVIEWING

A. Have students activate background knowledge in pairs by sharing what they know about special effects. If time permits, have pairs each share one or two examples of special effects with the class.

B. Play the video. Tell students to think about their discussion for question 1 as they watch. Does Abrams agree with their answers?

1. Abrams's TV shows and movies range from action to drama to science fiction.; **2.** His love of mystery was inspired by his interest in magic as a child and his trip to a magic store with his grandfather.; **3.** He says he likes magic that feels grounded, real, and tangible.

PART 1

Predicting

Answers will vary. The box is filled with different magic tricks sold at the store where Abrams bought it with his grandfather. Abrams explains that he has never opened the box.

Understanding Key Details

1. b; **2.** a; **3.** b

Critical Thinking

For Abrams, the mystery connected to the box's contents is more powerful than the actual contents themselves. The box now reminds him of the power and magic of mystery.

PART 2

Previewing

A. 1. Answers will vary. Digital technology and computer graphics make almost any visual effect possible these days.; **2.** Answers will vary. Abrams believes the technology that is available to all of us today makes movie-making accessible to anyone.

Understanding Key Details

A. 1. b; **2.** b

B. 1. He is referring to filmmakers who didn't get financial backing to make their films, and so their creative ideas have never been shared or seen by others.; **2.** The technology that we have access to now is enough to make good films.

PART 3

Previewing

We can infer that the movie has a lot of visual effects. *Mission: Impossible III* is both an action and science fiction movie set in the future.

Analyzing Problems and Solutions

A. Problem: An actor was being hurt in a movie scene when another actor pushed a gun up his nose. **Solution:** Abrams painted the actor's hand to look like the other's and let him push the gun up his own nose. The audience cannot tell the difference, and the actor is not in pain.

B. Abrams's solution is a simple one, one that he explains he could have thought of as a child with a very basic camera.

Critical Thinking

It is likely that Abrams would disagree with the main ideas of the reading passage. In his opinion, technology is not limiting us but providing us with more opportunities to create imaginative stories.

UNDERSTANDING KEY DETAILS

A. Have students work individually to complete the activity before checking answers as a class.

B. Give students a minute to work individually to read the excerpts and think about their answers to the questions before discussing in pairs. For question 2, elicit a class discussion. Ask students whether they agree with Abrams or not. Encourage them to give examples and reasons to support their opinions.

PART 3

PREVIEWING

Have students read the excerpt. Then elicit a class discussion to have students share background knowledge about the movie. If students are not familiar with the movie, have them work in pairs to go online and find some information about it to bring back and share with the class. *Extension:* Elicit a list of questions or key information about the movie that students will need to research. Give each pair one or two questions to answer or key pieces of information to find online. Then have each pair report back to the class.

ANALYZING PROBLEMS AND SOLUTIONS

A. Play the video. Have students work individually to answer the questions before checking answers as a class.

B. Have students discuss their thoughts in small groups. Ask them to come up with other possible low-tech solutions for Abrams's problem.

CRITICAL THINKING

Synthesizing. Review the reading passage in Lesson A by eliciting the key details from the class. Then have students discuss the questions in pairs or small groups.

EXPLORE MORE

Abrams also has a card game called the Mystery Box. Have students search online for more information about this game and how it helps inspire imagination.

Project — CREATING A STORY TO PRESENT

PROJECT OVERVIEW:

Aims:
- Students consider how a story could be told using the technology that is readily available to them.
- Students create an outline of a story and make a scene to present to the class.
- Students present their ideas and scenes to the class, assessing the usefulness of the technology they used.

Summary: Following on from J.J. Abrams's claim that modern technology allows anyone to make a movie, students attempt to create an outline, and a scene, of a story to present to the class.

Materials: computer/smartphone/tablet, Internet access, apps for making videos

Language Support: Using visuals in a presentation: *You can see in this video . . . ; Here you can see what we mean . . . ; Here's an example of . . . ; We'd like to show you an example of what we're talking about . . .*

TEACHING NOTES

PREPARATION

Have students work in pairs. Give them a few minutes to brainstorm some story ideas. If necessary, have a class brainstorming session to get some basic storylines that students can then work from. Encourage students to think about stories with action and mystery, such as the kind that J.J. Abrams makes. Note that the aim of the project is for students to use limited technology to create a piece of art. It does not have to be a video. Students can also draw pictures or make a sound recording. Note the "Language Support" phrases on the board and review them before students begin the activity.

DURING THE PROJECT

Give pairs enough time to explore the technology they are using and the apps available to them for their presentation and movie. Point out that not all useful apps will be video-related. For example, they may want a soundtrack for their movies and will need a music-making app if so. Explain that students' presentations should be about how they are going to make their movies using the technology that they have available to them. Then students can also include a scene from their movies as an example. Note that the latter will allow students to experiment creatively with their "mystery boxes," so if possible, create time in the lesson to allow for this.

AFTER THE PROJECT

Have groups discuss each other's presentations. Ask them to decide which idea they found most interesting and which is the most possible with the available technology. Have students comment on which movie or piece of art they'd most like to see more of. Take a class vote. Encourage students to give each other suggestions about how to improve their ideas and/or make better use of the technology available to them. *Extension:* Have students make part or all of their stories and present them to the class.

HOPE AND EQUALITY

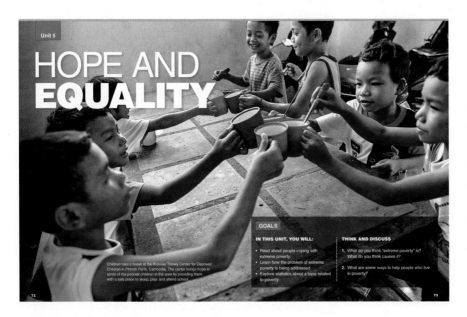

UNIT OVERVIEW

Reading: Students read about a photographer hoping to motivate people to do something about extreme poverty.

TED Talk: Musician Bono talks about the progress being made in reducing poverty and what we can continue to do until extreme poverty is completely eradicated.

Project: Students create and present an infographic on a topic related to poverty.

 **LIVING ON A DOLLAR A DAY**

LESSON OVERVIEW

Aims:
- Read and comprehend an interview with a photojournalist who uses her pictures to expose and fight extreme poverty in the world.
- Understand key details.
- Paraphrase information.

Target Vocabulary: access, circumstance, compassion, eradicate, goodwill, implication, intimate, overwhelmed, struggle, unexpected

Reading Passage Summary: Students read an interview with photographer Renée C. Byer, who has traveled to four continents to capture extreme poverty in her pictures. Byer's focus is not on the poverty as much as on the real people experiencing it. She focuses on domestic scenes—scenes that can connect viewers with the subjects in the photographs. In the interview, she talks about two of her well-known pictures, one taken in Liberia and the other in India, and the circumstances in which each was taken.

Then she talks about how she hopes her pictures move people to take action to end poverty worldwide.

TEACHING NOTES

THINK AND DISCUSS

This unit focuses on the problem of extreme poverty and what is being done to solve it. Point students to the map and caption on pages 74–75 for a better perspective. Extreme poverty, also known as absolute poverty, refers to a situation where basic needs are not met in daily life. The map shows how many people in the world live off of less than three dollars a day or 1,000 dollars a year. Have students share their ideas in pairs before eliciting a class discussion. Write a concept map on the board of students' ideas for question 2.
Extension: Ask students to share any personal experiences encountering extreme poverty in their home countries or while traveling. Tell them to share how they felt in addition to details of what they saw or experienced.

Think and Discuss

1. Answers will vary. Extreme poverty refers to a situation where even basic needs are not being met—a situation where there is no shelter, no sustenance, no safe water to drink, no access to healthcare, etc.; **2.** Answers will vary. Possibilities include: volunteer with organizations that help those in poverty, donate money, learn more about extreme poverty, educate others, etc.

Pre-reading

A. 1. parts of Africa and Asia; **2.** They earn less than $995 a year. The poorest live off of less than one dollar a day.

B. Answers will vary. It is clear that the people in the pictures have hard lives. The boys spend their days working at a garbage dump instead of going to school. The disabled mother works hard doing tough jobs every day to keep her daughter and herself alive. Note that the pictures also show connection, love, and even joy in the faces of these individuals, despite all the hardships in their daily lives.

C. 1. She is a photographer who depicts scenes of extreme poverty in her work.; **2.** She traveled to four continents to take pictures of extreme poverty. She hopes her images help others connect with and feel compassion for those living in poverty.

Getting the Main Ideas

The following should be checked: 2, 3, 5.

Understanding Key Details

A. Jestina: She lives in her neighbor's home; She washes laundry, sells cookies, and begs for money; She has a physical disability; **The little boy:** He lives on a garbage dump; His living space is 10 feet by 10 feet, and it is taken up by a bed for his family; He collects items/scavenges at a garbage dump in the slums.

B. Byer says that she is most affected by seeing the home life of the people she photographs. She is interested in finding pieces of daily life that others can connect with.

Paraphrasing Information

1. a; **2.** b; **3.** a

Building Vocabulary

A. 1. eradicate; **2.** access; **3.** implications

B. 1. c; **2.** e; **3.** a; **4.** d; **5.** b

C. 1. for; **2.** with; **3.** by; **4.** for

Getting Meaning from Context

A. 1. b; **2.** b

B. Answers will vary.

Critical Thinking

1. Byer hopes that the people who read her book are moved to take action to help people in situations of extreme poverty. She hopes her readers recognize themselves in the domestic scenes that she portrays, and as a result, feel a connection and a desire to help. **2.** Answers will vary.

PRE-READING

A. Focus students on the map key and elicit what the colors, and the different shades of the colors, represent. Darker shades indicate areas of low population density. The dark gray areas of the map are therefore places where very few people live, such as deserts. Students should be able to identify the areas in the lightest shades as major cities. Give students a few minutes to work individually to look closely at the map and answer the questions. Check answers as a class. Ask students whether the poorest countries surprised them or not. *Extension:* Focus a longer class discussion on the second part of question 2: Do you think you could live on this amount? Ask students to comment on what would be challenging about

having this little money. Use this to segue into a discussion for Exercise B.

B. Have students work in pairs. Give them one minute to look over the pictures. Tell partners to make a list of some of the challenges that the individuals in the pictures likely face in their daily lives. Refer students back to the map on pages 74 and 75 and ask them to find the locations pictured on page 77 (Delhi, India) and page 78 (Liberia).

C. Give students one minute to work individually to read the introduction and answer the questions. Check answers as a class. Ask students to share their initial opinions about Byer's work and pictures.

DEVELOPING READING SKILLS

GETTING THE MAIN IDEAS

Have students read the entire passage, either silently or while listening to the narrated passage on the audio. Have them work individually to complete the activity before checking answers in pairs. Point out that they should check three statements that summarize the main ideas expressed in the interview. *Extension:* Ask students to take one of the statements and share their thoughts. Tell them to work individually to write a paragraph to explain their opinions about the main ideas.

UNDERSTANDING KEY DETAILS

A. Have students work individually to complete the chart with details from the passage before checking answers in pairs. Encourage students to paraphrase information rather than copying details directly from the reading passage. Ask students to discuss what they think is the most challenging aspect about each individual's life.

B. Elicit a class discussion about what Byer focuses on in her photographs and why. Make sure students understand that connecting her audience to her subjects is important for Byer. *Extension:* Is Byer successful? Ask students if they feel connected to Jestina or the little boy when they see the pictures, and if so, why.

PARAPHRASING INFORMATION

Have students work individually to complete the activity. Give them a few minutes to go back to the passage to read the sentences around the statements in the exercise. Have students check answers in pairs. Ask students to comment on which out of the three statements by Byer they found the most interesting, and why.

BUILDING VOCABULARY

A. Have students complete the activity individually before checking answers as a class. The verb *eradicate* has a strong tone and is often used in reference to very serious problems. Nouns that collocate with *eradicate* include *disease*, *hunger*, *crime*, and *terrorism*. *Extension:* Ask students to write a three-sentence summary of the information about poverty and energy in Exercise A. Tell them to use as many vocabulary items as possible.

B. Have students complete the activity individually before checking answers in pairs. Drill the pronunciation of the vocabulary items, highlighting the stressed syllables.

C. Have students work individually to complete the activity before checking answers as a class. Write the verbs and prepositions on the board. Elicit additional example sentences.

GETTING MEANING FROM CONTEXT

A. Have students work individually or in pairs to complete the activity before checking answers as a class. Elicit example sentences for each phrase. *Extension:* Have students search for example sentences online to see the terms in use. Ask them to explain the meaning of the sentence to a partner.

B. Have students work individually to answer the questions before discussing in pairs or small groups. Encourage students to use the target vocabulary in their discussions. *Extension:* Have students work in pairs to write a summary of the TV show or movie that they discussed in question 2. Ask them to then comment on whether the show does an accurate job of portraying poverty and connecting viewers to the situation. Then have them share their summaries and opinions with the class.

CRITICAL THINKING

Interpreting. Elicit or explain the meaning of "call to action." Give students a few minutes to think about and write their answers before eliciting a class discussion. *Extension:* Ask students to also consider and discuss how poverty is portrayed in the media and how Byer's photos differ.

EXPLORE MORE

Have students search for images individually and then share one with a small group. Ask group members to discuss the emotional impact each image has on them personally. Which is the most effective?

THE GOOD NEWS ON POVERTY (YES, THERE'S GOOD NEWS)

LESSON OVERVIEW

Aims:
- Watch and understand a talk by musician Bono, who shares positive statistics about how global poverty is decreasing.
- Understand graphs and problems and solutions.
- Summarize main ideas.

TED Talk Summary: In his TED Talk, U2 lead singer Bono discusses current statistics on poverty and how they show improvement. He calls himself a "factivist," an evidence-based activist. Highlights of the information he shares include a 75-percent reduction in malaria deaths and the number of people living in extreme poverty being halved since 1990. Bono talks about using facts to create positive change and how technology helps us to both spread the word and to fight corruption. An annotated transcript for the edited TED Talk is on pages 82–83 of this Teacher's Guide.

TEACHING NOTES

The paragraph and questions introduce Bono the rock star and Bono the activist. His organization, ONE, is working hard to eradicate extreme poverty and educate the public through what he calls "factivism." Have students work individually to read the paragraphs and answer the questions. Encourage them to also use the background information that they learned about extreme poverty in Lesson A. Check answers as a class, eliciting students' thoughts and opinions about the facts that Bono shares. To give students a better understanding of Bono's celebrity status, ask students who are familiar with Bono and U2 to share any additional background information with the class. *Extension:* Have students work in pairs to go online and find out more about Bono, his music, or ONE. Then have pairs report back to the class on what they learned.

PART 1

PREVIEWING

Give students a minute to read the paragraph carefully. If necessary, elicit or explain the meaning of "drives me nuts." Check answers as a class. *Extension:* Ask students to come up with some reasons why we don't

know the "good news" about poverty. Encourage a discussion about the way poverty is portrayed in the media.

UNDERSTANDING MAIN IDEAS

Play the video. Ask students to circle the correct words as they listen. Point out that the information is a summary of what Bono says, and not verbatim. Alternatively, have students complete the activity before they watch the video. Then have them check their answers as they watch.

UNDERSTANDING GRAPHS

Have students look at the graph on page 85. Elicit what the axes represent. The x axis shows the year, and the y axis shows the percentage of people living in extreme poverty. Then give students a few minutes to work individually to answer the questions. Check answers as a class.

CRITICAL THINKING

Analyzing. Give students a couple of minutes to think about their answers. Encourage them to write notes, perhaps as a concept map, to support their discussion. Then have students work in small groups to share their ideas about getting to the zero zone. Have groups share some of the most plausible or intriguing ideas with the class. *Extension:* Take a class poll to see if students believe the zero zone will be reached or not. Then ask them to support their opinions with reasons.

PART 2

UNDERSTANDING PROBLEMS AND SOLUTIONS

A. Have students work individually to read the paragraph and answer the questions. Have students check answers in pairs. Ask pairs to paraphrase what Bono is saying in the excerpt. Elicit an explanation and examples of transparency. *Extension:* Have students work in pairs to go online and learn more about the connection between oil companies, Oslo, and corruption.

B. Have students quickly look over the list of problems and solutions. Then play the video. Check answers as a class. Elicit more detailed explanations about each

1. Bono is the lead singer of the rock band U2. His celebrity status as a rock star gives him influence and access to a large audience.; **2.** Since 2000, the following have happened: 8 million more AIDS patients are getting life-saving drugs; Eight countries in Africa have cut death rates from malaria by 75 percent; Childhood mortality rates are down by 2.65 million per year.

PART 1

Previewing

c

Understanding Main Ideas

reducing, halved, high

Understanding Graphs

1. The graph shows how extreme poverty is declining and may continue to decline in the near future.; **2.** The trajectory refers to the curve on the graph, which represents the future continued decline of extreme poverty.; **3.** If the decline continues at the same rate as now, by 2028 there will be no more extreme poverty. This is the zero zone.

Critical Thinking

Answers will vary.

PART 2

Understanding Problems and Solutions

A. 1. b; **2.** He says that oil companies are hiding data about money they pay to governments. The following should be underlined: oil companies are fighting to keep secret their payments to governments for extracting oil in developing countries.

B. Problems: d, c, f

Solutions: e, b, a

Summarizing Main Ideas

b

Critical Thinking

1–2. Answers will vary.

---

problem and solution. Ask students to talk more about what Bono means.

SUMMARIZING MAIN IDEAS

Have students work individually to complete the activity before checking answers as a class. Ask students to give more detail to the summary by adding information from the chart in Exercise B of **Understanding Problems and Solutions.**
Extension: Have students write a one-sentence summary of this part of the talk before they look at the exercise. Then have them compare their summaries to the correct one in the student book.

CRITICAL THINKING

Analyzing/Evaluating. Give students time to think alone before brainstorming in pairs. Both Byer and Bono are trying to affect people's attitudes and actions about extreme poverty, although their methods of approaching this task are rather different. Point out that while Bono is an artist in his other career, as an activist he prefers using facts to change people's thinking and actions.

CREATING AND PRESENTING AN INFOGRAPHIC

PROJECT OVERVIEW:

Aims:

- Students work in pairs to create an infographic about poverty.
- Students research relevant statistics and use them to design an infographic.
- Students present and explain their infographics to the class.

Summary: Students do further research into one area of poverty, focusing on statistics that show changes in that area over a time period. Students create an infographic to teach this information and present it to the class. The class then discusses what they learned from each other about poverty.

Materials: computer, Internet access, presentation software or posters and colored pens

Language Support: Presenting Statistics: *This infographic contains data about . . . ; The data tells us . . . ; The trend we see over time is . . .*

TEACHING NOTES

PREPARATION

Ask pairs to look over the list of suggested topics on page 87. Encourage them to choose a topic that interests them so they enjoy the research process and are motivated to find interesting statistics. Monitor students' topic choices, making sure there are a variety of topics represented. Then give pairs enough time to find statistics related to their topic. Some websites that may be useful in students' research include: nationalgeographic.com, data.worldbank.org, fao.org, globalissues.org. Note the "Language Support" phrases above on the board and review them before students begin the activity.

DURING THE PROJECT

Ask students to go back to the infographic that Bono presented to look at how the information was communicated. Point out that they can use this infographic for ideas and inspiration. Explain that a successful infographic has good information and is easy to understand. Encourage them to come up with their own ideas on how to make a successful infographic. Then tell partners to prepare a presentation to show the infographic and talk about the relevance of the information in it. Give pairs a few minutes to practice their presentations. Then have pairs form groups of three and take turns presenting to each other.

AFTER THE PROJECT

While pairs are presenting, remind other group members to listen carefully and take notes. Point out the discussion questions in **C** that students should be thinking about while listening to each other's presentations. After all groups have presented, elicit a class discussion about what students learned. Ask students to comment on surprising information or information that changed their thinking. *Extension:* To encourage further discussion, ask students to also evaluate the infographics and discuss which ones were most successful. Use the student-led learning style discussed in Unit 3.

EXPLORE MORE

ONE.org is focused on issues affecting people living in extreme poverty, including infectious diseases, maternal and child health, agriculture, and transparency.

Unit 6

BACKING UP HISTORY

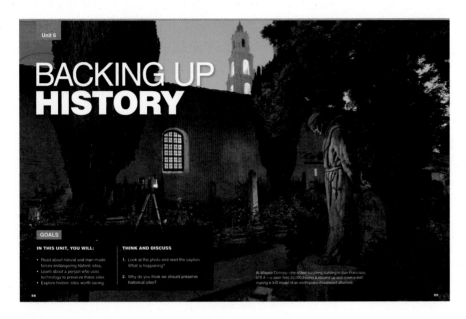

UNIT OVERVIEW

Reading: Students read about the work of CyArk, an organization that creates detailed digital records of cultural heritage sites.

TED Talk: CyArk founder Ben Kacyra shares examples of his organization's work and discusses the importance of preserving historical sites.

Project: Students choose an important cultural site for CyArk to preserve.

Lesson 6A | LASER PRESERVATION

LESSON OVERVIEW

Aims:

- Read and comprehend an article about how scanning technology is helping to preserve cultural heritage sites.
- Summarize key details.
- Understand a process.

Target Vocabulary: deteriorate, heritage, incorporate, intensity, occur, preserve, sacred, site, symbolic, thereby

Reading Passage Summary: Students read about the deterioration and destruction of important cultural heritage sites and how one organization is attempting to change this. Ben Kacyra, a pioneer in scanning technology, has founded an organization whose mission is to scan and record detailed digital records of sites around the world with historical and cultural value. The passage focuses on three such sites in different parts of the world and explains how CyArk is helping to preserve them: Rosslyn Chapel, the Eastern Qing Tombs, and Mount Rushmore.

TEACHING NOTES

THINK AND DISCUSS

This unit focuses on the work CyArk is doing to preserve historical sites across the world. For question 1, give students time to look over the photograph and read the caption. Ask students to paraphrase what the caption says. Elicit both an explanation of what is happening and why it is happening. Point out that the caption says that Mission Dolores is "earthquake-threatened." Elicit the meaning of this phrase and its significance in connection to what is happening. For question 2, have students discuss in pairs before eliciting a class discussion. Write a mind map on the board of ideas that students can refer to during discussion activities in the lesson. ***Extension:*** Ask students to share with a partner one important historical site from their home countries. Tell them to give as much information as they can about the site.

41

Think and Discuss

1. The picture shows 3-D imaging being taken of Mission Dolores, the oldest building in San Francisco, California.; **2.** Answers will vary.

Pre-reading

A. 1. The photo shows an actual picture of the Royal Kasubi Tombs in Uganda next to a digital scan taken of the site.; **2.** Answers will vary. The passage talks about a company using 3-D scanning technology to help preserve important cultural heritage sites.

B. 1. Scotland, China, U.S.; **2.** c, a, b; **3.** Guesses will vary. Each place is an important cultural heritage site that is being digitally preserved with the help of CyArk's advanced scanning technology.

Getting the Main Ideas

A. preserve, technology/scanning technology

B. Paragraph 3: 2; **Paragraph 4:** 2

Summarizing Key Details

The completed mind maps should appear as:

Rosslyn Chapel: Scotland, built in 15th century, includes mapping of symbolic carvings, pillars

The Eastern Qing Tombs: China, built in 17th century, site includes tombs of five Qing Dynasty emperors and 15 empresses

Mount Rushmore: U.S.A., built in 1941, represents the heads of four different American presidents

Understanding a Process

A. 1. d; **2.** e; **3.** b; **4.** g; **5.** f; **6.** a; **7.** c; **8.** h

B. images/models/scans; scanners/laser scanners; dimensions

Building Vocabulary

A. 1. sites; **2.** preserving; **3.** thereby; **4.** heritage; **5.** deteriorate

B. 1. a; **2.** c; **3.** c; **4.** a; **5.** b

C. Answers will vary.

Getting Meaning from Context

A. 1. c; **2.** a

B. Answers will vary.

Critical Thinking

1–3. Answers will vary.

PRE-READING

A. Have students work in pairs to look at the picture, read the caption, and read the first paragraph of the reading on page 90. Tell them to discuss the questions and their predictions about the passage.

B. Give students less than one minute to scan the information on page 92. Have them work individually to answer the questions. Check answers as a class. For question 3, ask students to also think about if their answers to Exercise A have changed at all after scanning more of the passage. *Extension:* Elicit more ideas about the passage content based on the unit title and lesson title.

DEVELOPING READING SKILLS

GETTING THE MAIN IDEAS

A. Have students read the entire passage, either silently or while listening to the narrated passage on the audio. Have them work individually to complete the summary.

B. Have students work individually to answer the questions before checking answers as a class. Note that while all the options may be true, only one sentence expresses each paragraph's main idea. *Extension:* The passage says that CyArk has already scanned 40 of the intended 500 sites. Ask students to go online and find updated figures. How many sites has CyArk scanned now? Make it a race to find the answer.

SUMMARIZING KEY DETAILS

Tell students to scan page 92 again to find the information to complete the mind map. Encourage them to do it first based on what they remember, and then to scan for any remaining information. Check answers as a class, focusing particularly on the last box for each site. Note that in the last box, students are asked to find varying information for each site. *Extension:* Have students work in pairs to share which site of the three in the passage they'd like to visit and why.

UNDERSTANDING A PROCESS

A. and B. Make sure students understand that the exercise refers to the information in the sidebar **Mapping a Monument** on page 93. Give students two minutes to read the information again. Have them work individually to complete the activity before checking answers in pairs. Then elicit answers, writing a mind map or infographic on the board to review the process. *Extension:* Have students work in pairs to summarize the process in their own words. Ask each pair to share their summary with the class. Have the class check if the summaries are correct or not.

BUILDING VOCABULARY

A. Have students complete Exercise A individually before checking answers as a class. The verb *preserve*, meaning "to keep something in its original condition," is a key word for this unit. Note that both a physical item like a photograph can be preserved and kept from damage, while an intangible thing like the past can also be preserved by helping to keep it alive or relevant. The word contains the prefix *pre-*, meaning "before," and *serve*, meaning "to keep." Another key word in the unit is the noun *heritage*, which comes from the verb *inherit*. Our heritage is something received from previous generations. It is something that is part of our history, either personally or on a wider scale as a nation or species. *Extension:* Have students share with a partner about a world heritage site in their home countries. Tell students to use the target vocabulary to talk about the site and its condition. If necessary, have students quickly search online to find out more about world heritage sites in their countries.

B. Have students complete Exercise B individually before checking answers as a class. Note that *incorporated* is also commonly paired with the preposition *in*.

C. Give students a minute to look over the questions and think about their examples. Then have them work in pairs to discuss and share their examples. Tell them to make a list of the objects they discuss. Elicit answers, encouraging a class discussion about symbolic objects that students know or use. *Extension:* Tell students to write a detailed description of a symbolic object they know, incorporating as much target vocabulary as possible into the paragraph.

GETTING MEANING FROM CONTEXT

A. Have students work individually to go back to the passage to find the terms and study the context of each. Check answers as a class, eliciting a more detailed explanation of *collective memory* to support Exercise B.

B. Give students a minute to read the question and think about their examples before having them discuss in pairs. Note that this exercise will also work well with small groups. Encourage students to share both the story and its significance. *Extension:* Have students write the story before sharing it with their partners or groups.

CRITICAL THINKING

Reflecting. Give students one minute to read the questions and think about their answers. Then elicit a class discussion to hear students' opinions, or have them share their answers in pairs.

EXPLORE MORE

National Geographic has various features on world heritage sites in the Travel section of their website. *Extension:* Have students learn more about the history and background behind world heritage sites by reading the "About" section at whc.unesco.org.

ANCIENT WONDERS CAPTURED IN 3-D

LESSON OVERVIEW

Aims:
- Watch and understand a talk about CyArk, an organization helping to preserve heritage sites.
- Identify benefits.
- Understand causes and effects.

TED Talk Summary: In his TED Talk, CyArk founder Ben Kacyra shares the story of how the organization was started and shows examples of some of the work it has accomplished. The laser scanning technology that CyArk uses was originally designed as a surveying tool. CyArk has completed more than 50 projects worldwide, some of which Kacyra shows examples of during his talk. He also speaks in detail about how the technology is being used not only to preserve, but to help educators, researchers, and students. An annotated transcript for the edited TED Talk is on pages 84–85 of this Teacher's Guide.

TEACHING NOTES

The information and questions here introduce more about Ben Kacyra and his organization CyArk, building on the knowledge that students gained in Lesson A. Give students two minutes to read the paragraphs and answer the questions. Have students check answers in pairs. *Extension:* Have students work in pairs to go online to quickly browse CyArk's website. Ask them to share one interesting thing that they saw or learned with the class.

PART 1

PREVIEWING

Give students one minute to read the excerpt. If necessary, elicit or explain the meaning of *winged bulls.* Have students discuss in pairs before eliciting a class discussion to hear their ideas.

UNDERSTANDING KEY DETAILS

Tell students to check their answers and ideas from **Previewing** while watching the talk. Play the video. Then have students work individually to complete the sentences before checking in pairs. If necessary, go over any unknown vocabulary to help with students' comprehension. See the annotated transcript at the back of this Teacher's Guide.

Extension: Ask students to think of some possible other uses for Kacyra's scanning technology. Have them brainstorm some ideas in pairs before eliciting a class discussion.

CRITICAL THINKING

Interpreting. Give students a few minutes to discuss their ideas with a partner. Tell students to recall what they discussed in **Previewing** as well. If necessary, explain that Kacyra refers to his father as "the dad" instead of "my dad" because he is telling the story from the third-person point of view. Ask students why he might have chosen to do this. *Extension:* Ask students to write a story from their childhood to describe an encounter or a conversation that affected them deeply like Kacyra's experience with his father and the winged bulls. Encourage them to write from the third-person perspective.

PART 2

IDENTIFYING BENEFITS

Play the video. Then have students work individually to answer the questions before checking answers as a class. For question 1, ask students to share some ways in which the public might use the digital records and information that CyArk has. *Extension:* Have students go online to browse the public information that CyArk offers. Tell them to share with a partner what they read and saw.

CRITICAL THINKING

Applying. Give students a minute to think about their answer to the question before discussing with a partner. Ask them to brainstorm together a list of possible ideas. Then have each pair share their favorite idea with the class. Write their ideas on the board.

UNDERSTANDING CAUSES AND EFFECTS

Have students work individually to read the excerpt and complete the questions. If necessary, elicit or explain the meaning of *natural phenomena* and *take their toll.* Check answers as a class. If possible, write the mind map on the board for question 2. For question 3, elicit a class discussion about the importance of our collective memory and why it must be preserved. Remind students that they also discussed the topic in Lesson A.

1. To digitally preserve the world's cultural heritage sites; **2.** CyArk was developed from the laser scanning technology that Kacyra invented in the 1990s.; **3.** It is available online at cyark.org.

PART 1

Previewing

Kacyra tells the story from his childhood to highlight both the important role that historical sites play in the cultural heritage of a people, as well as his own personal connection to this belief, which helps explain part of the inspiration behind his work.

Understanding Key Details

1. b; **2.** c; **3.** a; **4.** a; **5.** b

Critical Thinking

He is explaining how our personal cultural heritage is connected to historical sites. These sites provide us with a real example of history, and the legacy of people and civilizations, which can still teach us many lessons today.

PART 2

Identifying Benefits

1. The information is used by conservators and researchers. It is also available to the public for use in education, cultural tourism, etc.; **2.** Possibilities that he talks about include: a 3-D viewer of the site, fly-throughs, 3-D models, mobile apps with narrative virtual tools, as well as assistance with reconstruction of heritage sites when necessary.

Critical Thinking

Answers will vary.

Understanding Causes and Effects

1. He says it's happening at a rapid rate, too quickly. The following should be underlined: we are losing the sites and the stories faster than we can physically preserve them; **2. Natural threats:** earthquakes, floods, tornadoes; **Human threats:** arson, urban sprawl, acid rain, terrorism, wars; **3.** With the loss of the sites, part of our collective memory goes as well. And Kacyra explains that this collective memory is our collective treasure that we should be passing on to future generations, which is why it's important to save.

EXPLORE MORE

Note that students will have to search and read carefully to find the oldest site listed on cyark.org. Make it a competition between pairs by turning it into a race. The oldest site CyArk is working with is the Rock Art sites of Somaliland. *Extension:* Have pairs work to make a three-question quiz based on information on the site. Then have them give their quizzes to another pair.

RECOMMENDING A HISTORICAL SITE TO PRESERVE

PROJECT OVERVIEW:

Aims:
- Students choose a heritage site that they think should be preserved using CyArk technology.
- Students create an informative and visual presentation for their classmates about the site.
- Students discuss which site is most worthy of preservation.

Summary: Students create a proposal for CyArk's next project. Pairs choose a site, then create a presentation with information and visuals to convince their classmates that it is an important site to preserve. Pairs present to two other pairs and then reflect on the presentations and decide which site should receive the funding to be digitally preserved.

Materials: computer, photos or video footage, editing software, presentation software

Language Support: Persuasive language: *We strongly believe that . . . ; I think you'll agree that . . . ; It's undeniable that . . .*

TEACHING NOTES

PREPARATION

Have students work in pairs. Encourage them to choose a site that they know of and feel a connection with. Point out that the site does not have to be a World Heritage Site. Give pairs enough time to research the site and collect the relevant information for their presentations. Remind students that they will have to persuade their audience that the site is a worthy candidate for CyArk's preservation technology. Tell them to use the questions on page 103 of the Student Book as a guide but to also add any other information that might help persuade their audience. Remind them to also get images or videos as they research. Note the "Language Support" phrases above on the board and review them before students begin the activity.

DURING THE PROJECT

Monitor as teams work together on their presentations. Give assistance or feedback when necessary. Remind students that they only have two minutes, so they need to choose the most relevant information to share with their audience. Tell pairs to practice their presentation at least once. Then divide the class into groups with three pairs each. As students present, remind those listening to take notes and think of questions.

AFTER THE PROJECT

Have a class discussion about the sites they learned about. Ask students to share their thoughts on which one is the most interesting, which one is the most threatened, which one is the most deserving of funding, etc. Encourage students to give reasons and examples for their opinions. After the discussion, take a class vote to see which site will receive the funding and be digitally preserved by CyArk. *Extension:* Extend the discussion to ask students if and how presentation styles affected their feelings about each site. Ask students to comment on what was effective about some of the presentations, and how others could be improved. What made some speakers or presentations more persuasive than others?

EXPLORE MORE

Have students complete a TED Talk Summary worksheet (see page 10 of this Teacher's Guide) as they watch the talks.

FOOD FOR ALL

UNIT OVERVIEW

Reading: Students read about how the food that feeds the world's population is produced and distributed.

TED Talk: Carolyn Steel talks about how the rise in urban living is affecting our connection and relationship with food.

Project: Students propose an idea for making a neighborhood Sitopia—a place centered around food.

Lesson 7A FEEDING NINE BILLION

LESSON OVERVIEW

Aims:
- Read and comprehend an article about food being one of the biggest causes of global environmental problems.
- Identify problems and solutions.
- Understand infographics.

Target Vocabulary: accelerate, dilemma, emit, inefficient, pose, precise, prosperity, simultaneously, unreliable, yield

Reading Passage Summary: Students read about how food production is contributing to environmental problems in the world. Agriculture is creating air and water pollution, using too much of the world's precious water, destroying biodiversity, and contributing to deforestation and loss of wildlife. As the world's population continues to grow, and people eat more meat-intensive diets, the environmental challenges created by agriculture will only worsen. The author offers five steps that can help halt the damage being done: stop agricultural expansion, grow more on the farms we have, use water and other resources more efficiently, eat less meat, and reduce the amount of wasted food.

TEACHING NOTES

THINK AND DISCUSS

The unit focuses on the food we eat, the price the environment pays in order for the world's population to be fed, and how we might be able to fix this growing problem. Students will learn about how the food they eat gets to their plates. Encourage students throughout the unit to reflect on their own habits in regards to food and how they might make changes in order to be a part of the solution. Have students work individually first to write a list of the foods they ate today. Then ask them to think about where that food came from. Have students discuss in pairs or elicit a class discussion. For question 2, have the class brainstorm a list of possible negative effects on the environment that food production might have.

Think and Discuss

1. Answers will vary.; **2.** Answers will vary. Possibilities include: contributing to carbon and greenhouse gas emissions, depleting water resources, adding to pollution, causing deforestation and destruction of wildlife habitats, etc.

Pre-reading

A. 1. soybeans (pages 104–105), turkeys (page 106), peanuts (page 107), potatoes (page 107); **2.** Answers will vary. Large-scale farms require a lot of resources, people, machinery, and land space. Smaller farms are often run by individuals in sustainable environments and are better able to make efficient use of resources and the natural landscape around them.

B. 1. Guesses will vary. Actual answer: the predicted world population in 2050; **2.** Answers will vary. Possibilities include: growing enough food, not wasting food, production, distribution; **3.** Guesses will vary. The author writes that agriculture is one of the world's greatest contributors to global warming due to greenhouse gas emissions and water usage. It is also a large contributor to the destruction of biodiversity due to unnecessary land clearing and the destruction of habitats for wildlife.

C. The section contains suggestions for how to fix our dependency on agriculture and lessen its destructive impact on the environment.

Getting the Main Ideas

2

Understanding Problems

A. Clockwise from top: water supplies, polluter, fertilizer and manure, areas of grassland and forest, habitat and wildlife, cattle and rice farms, global warming/greenhouse gas emissions

B. 1. a; **2.** a; **3.** c

Identifying Solutions

1. d, g; **2.** c, j; **3.** e, b; **4.** f, a; **5.** h, i

Paraphrasing Information

Possible answers: **Step 2:** The second step is to increase output from farms that are currently not producing enough. This will help make better use of existing agricultural land. **Step 3:** The third step is to look toward organic farming to learn how to better use resources. This will help cut down on overuse of water and chemicals. **Step 4:** The fourth step requires us to eat less meat and more vegetables as well as find more environmentally friendly ways to raise cattle for meat. This will help cut down on the amount of food required to grow to feed cattle for meat. **Step 5:** The fifth step is to cut down on the amount of food that gets thrown out in homes and restaurants, as well as food that goes bad due to transportation issues. This would help decrease the food being wasted to less than 50 percent.

Understanding Infographics

more, 46.5%, agriculture, double, erosion, less

Building Vocabulary

A. 1. prosperity; **2.** poses; **3.** emits; **4.** yields; **5.** simultaneously

B. 1. b; **2.** b; **3.** a; **4.** b; **5.** a

C. 1. b; **2.** a; **3.** c; **4.** a

Getting Meaning from Context

A. 1. b; **2.** c

B. a major driver

Critical Thinking

Answers will vary. On an individual level, Step 4 and Step 5 are both possible with changes to our daily lives.

PRE-READING

A. Give students one minute to look over the photos and read the captions before answering the questions. Elicit a class discussion about different ways of farming and producing food for question 2. Ask students to share whatever background information they have on the topic.

B. Have students work individually to read the introduction. If necessary, have students look up the meanings of *smokestacks*, *greenhouse gases*, *nitrous oxide*, *carbon dioxide*, *livestock*, *manure*, and *biodiversity*. Check answers as a class. For question 1, it may be useful to elicit the current population of the world to help students realize that "nine billion" refers to the world's future population. *Extension:* Ask students if these are issues that they've thought about before. Elicit a discussion on our awareness (or lack of awareness) of how food gets to the table so we can eat it.

C. Give students 20 seconds to skim the headings. Note that their answers will be guesses. Have students check their answers after they read the passage.

GETTING THE MAIN IDEAS

Have students read the entire passage, either silently or while listening to the narrated passage on the audio. Have them work individually to answer the questions for Exercise A before checking answers in pairs. Then have students return to Exercise C of **Pre-reading** to check their answers.

UNDERSTANDING PROBLEMS

A. Point out that the activity is focused only on the content in paragraph 1. Have students work individually or in pairs to complete the map before checking answers as a class. Write the concept map on the board as you check answers. Refer back to it in **Identifying Solutions**.

B. Point out that the activity is focused on content in paragraph 2 and the infographic. Give students enough time to look over the infographic in detail. Have them work individually to answer the questions before checking answers in pairs. Note that question 1 asks about how many "additional" people we will need to feed. The current world population is 7 billion, and this is predicted to grow to 9 million by 2050. The correct answer is therefore *a*, 2 billion. *Extension:* Ask students if any of the information in either paragraph surprised them.

IDENTIFYING SOLUTIONS

Give students a few minutes to complete the chart before comparing answers in pairs. Check answers by connecting each solution to the relevant problem on the mind map from **Understanding Problems**. Ask students to comment on each solution and why they think it may be effective or not.

PARAPHRASING INFORMATION

Explain to students that they should be using their own words to explain each solution in more detail. Note that the example answer summarizes the action step in the first sentence and in the second sentence explains how that action will make a difference. Tell students they can use this same style of organization or another. Tell them to use the chart in **Identifying Solutions** as well as the mind map on the board to help them with their statements. Have students

compare answers in pairs. Ask students to look at the differences and similarities in their word choices and organization of ideas. Explain that paraphrasing and summarizing information like this is a useful tool in research as it forces readers to keep their writing in their own words from the start, helping them avoid plagiarism.

UNDERSTANDING INFOGRAPHICS

Give students a minute to work individually to complete the activity. Have them check answers in pairs. Ask students to share what piece of information in the infographic has impacted their thinking the most. *Extension:* Ask students to analyze and evaluate the infographic. Does it present the information well? Is it easy to understand?

BUILDING VOCABULARY

A. Have students complete Exercise A individually before checking answers as a class. Note that the verb *emit* is often used to talk about light, gas, or radiation.

B. Have students complete Exercise B individually before checking answers as a class. Something or someone that is *unreliable* can't be trusted or believed. Information can be unreliable, but so can a person. Unreliable people might break promises easily or not do what they say.

C. Have students work individually to complete Exercise C before checking answers in pairs.

GETTING MEANING FROM CONTEXT

A. Have students work individually before checking answers as a class. Elicit example sentences for each phrase. *Extension:* Have students work in pairs to go online and find more example sentences with each phrase.

B. Have students work individually to complete the sentence before checking answers in pairs.

CRITICAL THINKING

Evaluating. Have students discuss the questions in pairs before eliciting a class discussion for each. Encourage students to give reasons and examples for their opinions.

> **EXPLORE MORE**

Have students visit nationalgeographic.com and search for "future of food." Ask students to select an article to read and write a summary of it, paraphrasing the key information.

HOW FOOD SHAPES OUR CITIES

LESSON OVERVIEW

Aims:
- Watch and understand a talk about how city living affects people's relationship with food.
- Analyze arguments.
- Understand main and supporting ideas.

TED Talk Summary: In her TED Talk, food urbanist Carolyn Steel shares what she's learned about our changing relationship with food as the world's population becomes more urbanized. She focuses on our lack of connection to food and agriculture; we eat the food on our plates with no understanding of where it came from or how it got there. She believes this disconnect is contributing to a number of problems and that we cannot remain on this trajectory. She then talks about and suggests some ways to mend our relationship with food. She says that we need to create our own "Sitopia," places where food is important, valued, and understood. She shows some examples of how to do this, including farmer's markets, city gardens, and greenhouses where people grow food. Her hope is that food becomes a powerful tool that will shape our lives. An annotated transcript for the edited TED Talk are on pages 86–87 of this Teacher's Guide.

TEACHING NOTES

Have students work individually to read the paragraph and answer the questions. Note that the information here is from the full-length version of Steel's TED Talk. Check answers as a class. Ask students to share what the food industry is like in the cities in their home countries. Are their cities more connected to food than London? *Extension:* Point out that one of Carolyn Steel's titles on the page is *food urbanist*. Ask students to work in pairs to discover more about what this is. Have them search online and take notes. Ask them to think about how this works with her other professional title: *architect*. Tell each pair to report back what they learned to the class.

PART 1

PREDICTING

Explain that students will be guessing their answers. Have them work individually to complete the activity using any background knowledge they have. Play the video. Tell students to check their answers as they watch. *Extension:* Have a class discussion about the statistic in question 4. Why do they think so much food is wasted in the U.S.? What are their thoughts about this statistic?

UNDERSTANDING MAIN IDEAS

Give students a minute to read the statements and choose three. Check answers as a class, or play the video again to have students check their answers.

CRITICAL THINKING

Inferring. Give students two minutes to go back to the picture on pages 104–105 and to think about the connection between the soybean fields and the content of Steel's talk. Encourage students to also use the knowledge they gained in Lesson A. Have students first discuss in pairs before eliciting a class discussion. *Extension:* In her talk, Steel says that five corporations control 80 percent of global trade in food. Have students work in pairs to go online and find out more about one of these corporations. Ask each pair to report back what they learned about the corporation to the class.

ANALYZING ARGUMENTS

A. Have students work individually to complete the activity before checking answers in pairs. *Extension:* Tell students to go back to the three statements they chose in **Understanding Main Ideas.** Ask them to connect each of the statistics that Steel shares to a main point that it supports. Encourage them to find additional details from her talk to support each point.

B. Give students a few minutes to go back and review Foley's essay. Have them work individually to write their answers before eliciting a discussion. Both Foley and Steel agree that the current ways of the food industry are harmful to the planet and to our relationship with food. Ask students which individual they agree with more, and why.

PART 2

UNDERSTANDING MAIN AND SUPPORTING IDEAS

A. Note that students are guessing answers. Have them work individually or in pairs to read the excerpt and make guesses. Play the video. Tell students to

1. She thinks we can learn more about food and how it was produced and distributed by looking at how cities were organized. **2.** From the street names, we can see that each served a purpose in producing food 300 years ago (bread and chicken). **3.** Since we now mainly get food from supermarkets, often outside of the city, we've lost our connection with the food we eat.

PART 1

Predicting

Guesses will vary. Actual answers are: **1.** b; **2.** a; **3.** c; **4.** c

Understanding Main Ideas

The following should be checked: 1, 2, 5.

Critical Thinking

The photo illustrates how the natural landscape is being changed on a large scale to meet our changing food needs. That giant soybean farm is there to help feed all the animals that humans consume, so it also shows the effects of meat consumption.

Analyzing Arguments

A. third, ten, twice, 6 billion, 19 million, half, billion

B. 1. Answers may vary. Possibilities include: a third of the annual grain crop goes to cattle for raising meat;

it takes 10 times as much grain to feed a human if it's passed through an animal first; by 2050, twice as much dairy and meat will be consumed; 19 million hectares of rain forests are cleared each year, and 19 million hectares are also lost to erosion every year; half the food in the U.S. is thrown away; 80% of global food trade is controlled by five multinational corporations.; **2.** Both agree on the areas in which food production and agriculture are causing harm, and both agree that this problem is only going to get much worse in the coming decades.; **3.** Steel is much more focused on how urban living has affected food production negatively, while Foley does not focus as much blame on city living.

PART 2

Understanding Main and Supporting Ideas

A. Predictions will vary. The actual answers are: center, selling, water, smell, throw it.

B. The following should be checked: Food is at the center of family life.; People take time for food, and celebrate it.; Markets sell food that is fresh and grown locally.; Community projects educate children about food.; Cities and nature are seen as part of the same framework.

C. Answers will vary. Steel talks about farmers' markets and urban gardens as some examples.

check their answers as they watch. Elicit any guesses that were incorrect but that students believe would also work for the sentences. For example, other words that would work for the second answer include *making, cooking, eating, growing*.

B. If necessary, play the video again. Have students work individually to complete the activity, checking their answers in pairs. Point out that students should check five answers. ***Extension:*** Have students work in pairs to take one aspect of a Sitopia and discuss why it's important. Ask them to share their ideas with the class.

C. Give students one minute to think about their answer before sharing in pairs. Tell students to think about the aspects that they checked in Exercise B— How many aspects does their example of Sitopia have? Point out that these examples don't have to be official programs. It could simply be an example of a family making the effort to have a homemade dinner together every night.

EXPLORE MORE

Encourage students to also find out more about Steel's book *Hunger City: How Food Shapes Our Lives.*

PRESENTING A PROPOSAL

PROJECT OVERVIEW:

Aims:
- Students write a proposal for a Sitopia in their areas or communities.
- Students present their proposals to the class.
- Students analyze each other's proposals and make suggestions for improvements.

Summary: Students watch some TED Talks that share various examples of a Sitopia. Then pairs design their own plans to make a Sitopia in their communities. Students present their plans to each other and get feedback and ideas.

Materials: computer, presentation software or poster board/paper, marker/color pens

Language Support: Making and replying to suggestions: *Let's . . . ; How about . . . ; Sounds good!; I'm not sure . . . ; That's a good idea.*

TEACHING NOTES

PREPARATION

Have students work in pairs. Tell them to look over the titles of the TED Talks and focus on the ones that sound interesting to them. Encourage them to watch the talks, or have them skim the transcripts if time is an issue. Tell students to take notes as they watch or read and try to find inspiration for their own Sitopia ideas. Note the "Language Support" phrases above on the board and review them before students begin the activity.

DURING THE PROJECT

Tell students to go through the questions on page 119 as they brainstorm ideas for their Sitopia. Point out that their proposals should explain what their Sitopia is and how it contributes to reconnecting the community with food. Give students enough time to plan their two-minute presentations. Encourage them to use pictures or videos to give examples of their ideas, if possible. Have pairs practice their presentations once before finding two other pairs to work with. Remind the listeners to take notes and think about how each proposal can be improved.

AFTER THE PROJECT

Have group members share their impressions after each presentation. Encourage them to ask questions and make suggestions. After groups have completed giving their feedback, elicit a class discussion about all of the proposals. Ask students to talk about their favorite ideas. Use the questions on page 119 of the Student Book as a guide for the discussion. If possible, let students lead the discussion.

EXPLORE MORE

Have students search online to find out what areas are improving and which ones still need more improvement in their communities. Ask students to also share any personal experiences they have with a Sitopia.

FUTURE JOBS

UNIT OVERVIEW

Reading: Students are introduced to a supercomputer that's creating innovative recipes, illustrating how the evolution of technology may affect jobs in ways we didn't imagine.

TED Talk: Management theorist Andrew McAfee talks about how technology and robotics will change our workforce in the near future and discusses how we can make this a positive transition.

Project: Students create a poster about the future of automated jobs.

Lesson 8A RECIPES FOR INNOVATION

LESSON OVERVIEW

Aims:
- Read and comprehend an article about the supercomputer chef, Watson, and the implications this kind of advanced technology has for the future of jobs in general.
- Understand organization and purpose.
- Connect purpose to main ideas.

Target Vocabulary: capability, deduce, mission, niche, novel, obsolete, retain, routine, theme, unconventional

Reading Passage Summary: Students read about how supercomputer Watson is turning its talents to cooking and recipe creation. It's called cognitive cooking and involves generating a new recipe based on the computer's huge database of food ingredients, recipes, and flavor combinations. Giving this creative role to a computer brings into question the need for humans in certain fields of work. However, there are still some areas where humans are better than computers, such as pattern recognition, making

emotional connections, storytelling, and despite Watson's best efforts, even innovation.

TEACHING NOTES

THINK AND DISCUSS

This unit focuses on how automation is changing the workforce, in some cases in surprising ways, and how this may affect humans. For question 1, have students work in pairs to brainstorm a list of jobs that robots and computers can do instead of humans. Then elicit a class discussion to have students share some jobs on their lists and comment on which ones can be easily automated. Ask students to look at the picture and share about any similar type of robot that they've seen in action.

PRE-READING

A. Give students a minute to read the question and write their answers before discussing in pairs. Tell them to build off of the **Think and Discuss** discussion. Note that computers are typically not considered to be creative or innovative, but students will read about one that is.

Think and Discuss

1. Answers will vary. Possibilities include: production-related jobs, driving-related jobs, cleaning-related jobs, research-related jobs, assistants who organize schedules, etc.; **2.** Answers will vary. Jobs that are easy to automate probably contain more of a mechanical element than a creative one, such as jobs that already rely on machines now.

Pre-reading

A. 1. Answers will vary. Computers and machines are often more skilled than humans at calculations, measurements, and tasks that require precision. Robots are usually unable to do jobs that require innovative and creative thinking or spontaneous or instinctual decision-making. However, students will learn about a creative computer in the reading.

B. Answers will vary. Possibilities include:
Computer chef: cutting, chopping, frying, serving, recipe generation

Human chef: checking taste of dishes, presentation of food, interacting with customers

C. Answers will vary. Something or someone that is *obsolete* is outdated and no longer needed. If machines start to make and do things better than humans and therefore replace much of our workforce, they will make humans obsolete in regards to labor.

Understanding Organization and Purpose

A. 3

B. Section 1: d; **Section 2:** c; **Section 3:** g; **Section 4:** a; **Section 5:** f

Connecting Purpose to Main Ideas

Answers will vary slightly. Possibilities include:

Section 1: In recent years, computers are becoming more and more powerful.

Section 2: Similar to the human mind, Watson's mind works by making an educated guess based on his database of knowledge.

Section 3: Watson creates recipes by drawing on his database to come up with unconventional combinations.

Section 4: In the future, cognitive computing may be used in the healthcare, sales, or travel industries—all fields that require quick assessments of massive amounts of data.

Section 5: Humans are still better than computers when it comes to pattern recognition, emotional connections, innovation, and non-routine physical tasks.

Understanding Key Details

A. The following should be underlined: Watson's mission is to invent recipes that are both delicious and unconventional.

B. 35,000 recipes; flavor combinations; ingredients; the chemical combinations that create flavor

C. Aspects mentioned in the passage include: invent recipes, evaluate different combinations of ingredients, make healthy yet unconventional recipes.

Understanding a Main Message

A. 1. automation, welding/bank tellers/cashiers/typists/proofreaders; **2.** speed, efficiency; **3.** low risk

B. 1. jobs that involve creativity, social intelligence, non-routine physical activity, pattern recognition, emotional connections, innovation, storytelling; **2.** Answers will vary.

C. Answers will vary.

Building Vocabulary

A. 1. routine; **2.** capabilities; **3.** mission; **4.** deduce; **5.** obsolete

B. 1. e; **2.** b; **3.** d; **4.** a; **5.** c

C. 1. a, b; **2.** b, c; **3.** a, b; **4.** a, c

Getting Meaning from Context

1. b; **2.** b; **3.** c; **4.** b

Critical Thinking

Answers will vary. If computers replace humans on a large scale, it will leave many people without employment and a source of income. On the other hand, if computers take over menial labor, it may give people more time and freedom to pursue work that is more innovative, and help move the human race forward.

B. Give students 30 seconds to skim the passage. Ask them to use the headings as inspiration for their answers as well as add their own ideas. Elicit a class brainstorm to check answers as a class. ***Extension:*** When having students brainstorm, write a Venn diagram on the board. Ask them to also think about what tasks both a human and a computer chef can do.

C. Have students discuss their answers in pairs. If necessary, let them check the meaning of *obsolete* in a dictionary. Ask students to think about the kinds of jobs that humans may no longer need to do and the positive and negative results of this. ***Extension:*** Have students work in small groups. Ask them to design a robot to help them at school. What do they think that robot would be capable of helping with? Have groups present their ideas to the class. If time permits, have them make posters.

DEVELOPING READING SKILLS

UNDERSTANDING ORGANIZATION AND PURPOSE

A. Have students read the entire passage, either silently or while listening to the narrated passage on the audio. Have students read the information about purpose. Explain that the questions ask students to focus on the purpose of specific sections of the passage. Have them work individually to answer the questions for Exercises A and B before checking answers as a class.

B. Check answers as a class. Ask students to identify the lines in the passage that gave them clues about each section's purpose.

CONNECTING PURPOSE TO MAIN IDEAS

Have students work individually to write their answers before checking in pairs. Point out that students' wording will vary. Explain that learning to paraphrase main ideas is an important skill in research.

UNDERSTANDING KEY DETAILS

A. Have students work individually to underline the sentence before checking answers in pairs.

B. Have students work individually to complete the chart before checking answers as a class.

C. Have students work in pairs to add content to the charts on page 122. ***Extension:*** Ask students to comment on Watson's "creative process." Is he creating, or is he automating using his database? Tell students to support their opinions with examples and reasons.

UNDERSTANDING A MAIN MESSAGE

A. Point out that students should be using the content on page 125 to complete the sentences, including the sidebar below the text. Have students work individually to complete the activity before checking answers in pairs.

B. Have students work in pairs to answer the first question. Have them get in small groups to discuss their thoughts for question 2. Ask them to make a list of jobs that require those talents. Elicit some examples from each group.

C. Give students 30 seconds to write their ideas before discussing with a partner. Note that there is no mention in the article of Watson actually cooking the food, only creating the recipe. ***Extension:*** Have students go online to learn more about the food truck that is serving Watson's creations. Ask them to find out who is cooking.

BUILDING VOCABULARY

A. Have students complete Exercise A individually before checking answers as a class. ***Extension:*** Ask students to go online and find out more about Siri. Tell them to add to information they learned in the activity. Have pairs present to each other, using as many vocabulary items as possible.

B. Have students work individually to complete the activity before checking answers in pairs. Note that the noun *niche* usually refers to a special place or position in work or life. Students will see in Exercise C that *niche* is often used as a modifier, too, to describe a specialized area for businesses.

C. Have students work in pairs to complete the activity before checking answers as a class. Elicit or explain the meaning of each collocation. ***Extension:*** Elicit example sentences for each or have students write sentences.

GETTING MEANING FROM CONTEXT

Have students complete the exercise individually before checking answers as a class. Describing someone as "hands-on" can mean that they are active and involved in doing something, as well as actually physically using their hands or body. When used in regards to learning or teaching, the adjective usually indicates first-hand involvement. Someone who is "in your corner" is supporting you. The idiom likely comes from boxing, where the team that supports each opponent stands in that boxer's corner of the ring during a fight. ***Extension:*** Have students work in pairs to go online and find additional example sentences that use each expression. Have them introduce the sentences to another pair.

CRITICAL THINKING

Predicting. Give students a minute to think about and write their answers in the space provided. Then have them discuss their ideas in pairs. Encourage students to go back to their list of jobs for **Think and Discuss** as they discuss.

EXPLORE MORE

Have students search online for some examples of Watson's recipes. Elicit a few examples and write the ingredients on the board. Have students discuss their opinions of the recipes in pairs or small groups.

Lesson 8B WHAT WILL FUTURE JOBS LOOK LIKE?

LESSON OVERVIEW

Aims:
- Watch and understand a talk about how technology is changing our job opportunities.
- Identify trends.
- Understand solutions.

TED Talk Summary: In his TED Talk, management theorist Andrew McAfee talks about how we can best deal with the changes that automation is creating in the workforce. With the rise of information technology and intelligent computers, blue-collar workers are losing jobs, but McAfee says the good news is that this is creating an opening for many more entrepreneurs and innovators. He thinks this is positive for the human race, as long as society creates ways in which all kinds of people have access to the opportunity of better education and the chance to become creators. An annotated transcript for the edited TED Talk is on pages 88–90 of this Teacher's Guide.

TEACHING NOTES

The paragraph explains Andrew McAfee's work in regards to educating others about jobs and automation. Note that while the paragraph seems to imply that McAfee doesn't have a positive outlook on the future of jobs, students will hear in his talk that in fact he does. However, he says that societal changes have to be made to make the best-case scenario happen. Have students read the paragraphs individually before writing their answers. Then check answers as a class. For question 3, remind students that they learned in Lesson A about how Watson's cognitive computing might change patient diagnosis. Have them discuss more about how this might change a doctor's job, instead of making the job obsolete.

PART 1

PREVIEWING

Have students work individually to read the excerpt before discussing meaning in pairs. Tell students to check their answers as they watch in **Getting the Main Ideas**.

GETTING THE MAIN IDEAS

Have students quickly read over the answer choices. Then play the video. Tell them to circle the main idea while also checking their answers to **Previewing**. Ask students if any of the jobs they talked about in the previewing activity were mentioned by McAfee so far.

PART 2

PREVIEWING AND PREDICTING

Have students work individually to read the excerpt and answer the questions before comparing answers in pairs. Note that the answer to question 1 somewhat contradicts what students read about McAfee in the introduction, as he is positive here about the future of jobs. In this excerpt, he is talking specifically about creative people for whom technology is giving new resources for artistic expression in their work.

CRITICAL THINKING

Predicting. Give students a minute to think about their answers before eliciting a class discussion. Note that while McAfee is generally positive about the new machine age, he admits that if society doesn't make certain changes, there may be some negative effects.

1. He studies the way that information technology affects business and the larger society.; **2.** He says that artificial intelligence, sophisticated algorithms, and access to massive data allow intelligent machines to do complex work.; **3.** A computer might be able to diagnose a patient's illness more accurately and efficiently.

PART 1

Previewing

Answers will vary. He is referring to the automation of jobs. An example can be seen in the computer chef pictured in Lesson A.

Getting the Main Ideas

a

PART 2

Previewing and Predicting

1–3. Guesses may vary. Actual answers are:
1. McAfee is hopeful. He believes that the potential for human innovation is growing with technology.;
2. Examples of jobs that he mentions in Part 1 include driving jobs, customer service jobs, warehouse jobs. In Part 2, he talks about how technology will benefit craftsmen and artists.; **3.** He explains that technology will help craftsmen and artists create more easily, which will bring more innovation to society.

Critical Thinking

Answers will vary.

PART 3

Identifying Trends

A. For people like Ted, there has not been a large change in the hours that the head of household works. People like Ted have been relatively happy in their marriages over the years. In the last 10 years, they have even become happier in their marriages. For people like Bill, the heads of households are working less and there has been a sharp decline in happy marriages.

B. Guesses will vary. Actual answers are: Ted, Bill.

C. **1.** Ted; **2.** Bill; **3.** Ted; **4.** Bill; **5.** Bill

PART 4

Understanding Solutions

A. The following should be checked: 2, 3, 4, 6.

B. **1.** He believes technology is going to create more and more automation especially in blue-collar industries; we need to create schools that encourage more entrepreneurs and leaders than manual laborers.; **2.** a, d

Critical Thinking

Answers will vary.

PART 3

IDENTIFYING TRENDS

A. Give students a minute to look over the graphs. Explain that they should try to write one sentence each about Bill and Ted to summarize what the graph is saying before discussing with a partner. Check answers as a class. Make sure students understand how to read the graphs correctly.

B. Have students work in pairs to complete the activity. Play the video. Have students check their answers to A and B as they watch. *Extension:* Ask students to comment on whether or not these statistics seem true for the Bills and Teds in their home countries.

C. Have students work alone to complete the statements before checking answers in pairs. Then elicit a discussion about Bill and Ted. Ask students to summarize what they learned about each stereotype. Make a Venn diagram on the board to take notes on what students say to compare the two types of workers. *Extension:* Extend the discussion by asking students to consider how future automation might positively change the lives of people like Bill. This is what McAfee addresses in the last part of his talk.

PART 4

UNDERSTANDING SOLUTIONS

A. Have students look over the list quickly. Play the audio. Have students work individually to complete the activity before checking answers in pairs.

B. Give students time to read the excerpt and think about their answers. Have them work individually before eliciting a class discussion to check answers.
Extension: Have students work in small groups to brainstorm some additional ways to create more Teds in society.

CRITICAL THINKING

Personalizing. Give students time to think about their answer to the question. Have students discuss in pairs, giving reasons for their answers. Then encourage a class discussion to have students share their thoughts and opinions.

 **Project**

CREATING A POSTER ABOUT FUTURE JOBS

PROJECT OVERVIEW:

Aims:
- Students work in groups to make a poster about job automation in the future.
- Students present their posters to the class.
- The class discusses the similarities and differences between each group's poster.

Summary: Students create a poster that explains their ideas about when and how some jobs are going to become automated. Students are given a list of jobs to make predictions about. Groups discuss when and how each job will be automated and then make a poster that reflects the content of their discussion. Then groups present their posters to the class and the class compares and contrasts each other's ideas and predictions.

Materials: paper, pen, colored pens, poster board

Language Support: Talking about different topics: *Let me first focus on . . . ; Let's next talk about . . . ; Now let's look at . . .*

TEACHING NOTES

PREPARATION

Have students work in small groups. Tell them to look over the list of jobs and research any that they are unfamiliar with. Ask them to then share their thoughts and ideas about when these jobs will become automated. Tell them to use the questions on page 135 to guide their discussion. Note that they should decide the order in which the jobs may become automated and what aspects of each job may become automated. Monitor as groups discuss. Make sure students are taking notes during their discussion. Note the "Language Support" phrases above on the board and review them before students begin the activity.

DURING THE PROJECT

Monitor as groups work together to make their posters. Give assistance or feedback when necessary. Point out the list on page 135 of what should be on the posters: pictures, an estimated date of when the job will be automated, a description of how it will be automated. Tell groups to think about the best way to present this information. Encourage them to make the poster into a type of infographic. Give teams two minutes to practice their presentations before showing their posters to the class. Remind students to take notes while listening to each other's presentations and think of any questions or comments they might have. Tell students to form opinions about each other's posters while they're listening.

AFTER THE PROJECT

If necessary, give students time to study each other's posters in more detail. Then ask groups to discuss each of the posters and the information presented in them. Was there a range of ideas and predictions in the different posters? Which group's predictions sound most accurate? Have students ask questions and make comments on each other's ideas and predictions.
Extension: Turn the discussion to the posters. Which was the most effective in communicating the information, and why?

EXPLORE MORE

The blog summarizes two TED Talks about the future of work and innovation in the U.S. If time permits, have students work in pairs to watch one talk and take notes. Then have them report what they learned to a pair who watched the other talk.

HOW WE LEARN

UNIT OVERVIEW

Reading: Students read about current research into language acquisition in babies.

TED Talk: Patricia Kuhl talks about how babies learn and differentiate languages.

Project: Students write a blog post on raising bilingual children.

 ## WHAT BABIES KNOW ABOUT LANGUAGE AND WHY WE SHOULD CARE

LESSON OVERVIEW

Aims:
- Read and comprehend a review of two current research studies on language acquisition and infants.
- Understand purpose and sequence.
- Apply information.

Target Vocabulary: abuse, accustomed to, ban, barrier, discrimination, downside, eliminate, initially, instinctive, justify

Reading Passage Summary: Students read about what recent research is telling us about language acquisition at a young age. Psychologist Whitney Weikum conducted a study that concluded that babies can differentiate visually between languages. They notice the difference in shapes made by the mouth from four to six months of age. And Harvard's Katherine Kinzler examined how and when babies begin to develop linguistic preference. Both studies show that babies, before they can even speak, develop a preference for their own language and for speakers of that language. One downside is that this means language-based prejudice also develops in our minds at a very young age.

TEACHING NOTES

THINK AND DISCUSS

The unit explores recent research into brain development and language acquisition in babies. Encourage students to think about their own language-learning journey as they read through the unit. Have students discuss the questions in pairs.

PRE-READING

A. Give students two minutes to study the graph and answer the questions. Focus students' attention on the *y* axis, which represents the number of synapses (connections) in the brain. The number of synapses in the brain is connected to our ability to learn new information. Have students work individually to write

Think and Discuss

1–2. Answers will vary.

Pre-reading

A. 1. before our first birthday; **2.** As we become adults, our ability declines.; **3.** Answers may vary. The graph shows that, as adults, there are significantly fewer synapses, or connections, in our brains when we learn languages than when we learn as babies.

B. 1. Guesses will vary. In the research talked about in the passage, a baby's sensitivity to a language is assessed by studying how the babies react to people speaking different languages.; **2.** Answers will vary. Possibilities include: babies can understand simple words they hear; they can understand and use body language such as gestures, eye contact, head movement, as well as making sounds, crying, etc.

Getting the Main Ideas

3

Understanding Purpose and Sequence

A. 1. c; **2.** a

B. Weikum's Experiment: e, h, b, f, a

Kinzler's Experiment: d, g, i, c

C. 1. f; **2.** b; **3.** c; **4.** a; **5.** e; **6.** d

Applying Information

1. L, U; **2.** L, L; **3.** L, U; **4.** L, L; **5.** U, U

Building Vocabulary

A. 1. downside; **2.** Initially; **3.** accustomed to; **4.** instinctive; **5.** justify

B. 1. c; **2.** a; **3.** d; **4.** e; **5.** b

C. 1–2. Answers will vary.

Getting Meaning from Context

A. 1. b; **2.** a; **3.** a

B. Answers will vary.

Critical Thinking

1. It describes a time when governments made it illegal to speak minority languages in public places, including schools. In some cases, these languages then disappeared.; **2.** Answers will vary. The passage explains that we favor speakers of our own language instinctively, which may explain why some governments forced people, children especially, to speak the country's official language instead of their native languages.; **3.** The author is saying that although we might instinctually prefer speakers of our own language, it doesn't mean that we should allow ourselves to treat others badly as a result.

their answers, comparing in pairs. Ask pairs to discuss their thoughts and ideas, giving reasons or examples when possible. For question 3, have pairs share one of the ideas they discussed with the class.

B. Make sure students understand to answer the questions based only on the title of the reading: What Babies Know About Language and Why We Should Care. Have them work together in pairs to discuss and write their ideas. For question 2, ask students to think about how babies communicate before they are able to speak. Elicit a class discussion by asking for pairs to share some interesting points that they discussed.

DEVELOPING READING SKILLS

GETTING THE MAIN IDEAS

Have students read the entire passage, either silently or while listening to the narrated passage on the audio. Make sure they also read the sidebar text. Have them work individually to complete the activity before checking answers in pairs. *Extension:* Ask students to share their earliest memories of language learning.

UNDERSTANDING PURPOSE AND SEQUENCE

A. Have students work individually to complete the activity. Tell them to go on to Exercise B without checking answers.

B. Have students work individually to complete Exercise B before checking answers to A and B in pairs. Then ask pairs to summarize each of the research studies and their results in their own words before turning the page for Exercise C. *Extension:* Ask partners to talk about which study they find more interesting and why.

C. Have students work alone to complete the summary before checking answers in pairs.

APPLYING INFORMATION

Explain that students will have to read the instructions carefully, noting that the exercise refers to a child from a French-speaking home, and apply the information that they learned in the passage to infer the correct answers. Have students work individually to complete the chart before checking answers in pairs. *Extension:* Have students work individually to write two more statements to add to the chart. Ask them to give the statements for their partners to complete. Then have partners check each other's answers.

BUILDING VOCABULARY

A. Have students complete Exercise A individually before checking answers as a class. The noun *downside* refers to a negative effect of something that otherwise seems attractive or positive.

B. Have students complete Exercise B individually before checking answers in pairs. One definition of the verb *discriminate* means to "differentiate between two or more things." Another common meaning is "to treat someone unfairly because you consider them different." In this second meaning, the verb often appears as *discriminate against*.

C. Give students a minute to read the questions and think about their answers before having them discuss in pairs. Encourage students to use the target vocabulary in their discussions. *Extension:* Have students work individually to use the new vocabulary items to write a story about an experience that involves linguistic prejudice.

GETTING MEANING FROM CONTEXT

A. Have students work individually to complete Exercise A before checking answers as a class. Elicit additional example sentences for each expression.

B. Give students a minute to write their answers before eliciting a class discussion to check students' ideas. Ask students to support their opinions with examples and reasons. Tell students to use personal experience in addition to what they learned in Lesson A to support their ideas. *Extension:* Have students share their thoughts about the content of the passage using as many of the target vocabulary items from **Getting Meaning from Content** as possible.

CRITICAL THINKING

Interpreting. Give students a minute to reread the content of "Banned Languages." Have them work individually to answer the questions before discussing them in pairs. For question 3, elicit a class discussion on linguistic prejudice. Ask students to share any examples they know of banned language or similar linguistic prejudice by a government. *Extension:* To encourage more discussion, ask students to talk about how unconscious linguistic prejudice might negatively affect the way we interact with people from other cultures and nations. Does becoming aware of this prejudice change students' own thinking about anything?

EXPLORE MORE

If necessary, have students work in small groups to make a summary of the article together. Tell each group member to read a section of the article and then summarize it for the group.

Lesson 9B · THE LINGUISTIC GENIUS OF BABIES

LESSON OVERVIEW

Aims:
- Watch and understand a talk about babies and language learning.
- Understand visuals.
- Recognize tone and message.

TED Talk Summary: In her TED Talk, Patricia Kuhl shares her research findings in regards to infants and language acquisition. Kuhl concentrates on the critical period of language acquisition, and specifically how and when babies learn to recognize the sounds particular to their native languages. She has learned that babies under one are able to discriminate the sounds of all languages, whereas adults can only do this for their native languages. Before their first birthdays, babies are actually taking statistics on the sounds they hear, and as they absorb the statistics of the sounds they most frequently hear, their brains change. An annotated transcript for the edited TED Talk is on pages 91–92 of this Teacher's Guide.

TEACHING NOTES

The paragraphs introduce the general question about babies and language learning at the heart of Kuhl's research: Why are we better language learners as infants? Have students work alone to read the information and answer the questions. Check answers as a class. Note that students have met the phrase *critical age* in Lesson A. For question 3, ask them to compare *critical age* with *critical period*. **Extension:** Remind students that they read about two other studies in Lesson A. Have them compare the questions that each is trying to answer.

PART 1

PREVIEWING

Give students a few minutes to work individually to read the excerpt and think about their answers before discussing in pairs. If necessary, elicit or explain the meaning of *neuroscience*. Note that the term *rocket science* is used colloquially to describe something that is extremely complicated and difficult to understand. The term is often used in the negative to emphasize that something is simple or easy to understand: *It's not rocket science.*

GETTING THE MAIN IDEAS

Have students quickly look over the concept map. Play the video. Have students work individually to complete the concept map before checking answers in pairs. If necessary, elicit or explain the meanings of *purpose*, *methodology*, and *results* in regards to a research study.

CRITICAL THINKING

Interpreting. Give students a minute to think about their answers before discussing in pairs. Ask students to think about how they are culture-bound listeners themselves. Point out that Kuhl says that we are all culture-bound listeners as adults. Encourage students to think back to what they learned in Lesson A to discuss positives and negatives of this.

PART 2

UNDERSTANDING VISUALS

A. Give students time to look over the graphs. Have them work individually to answer the questions before watching the video. Then play the video. Ask them to check their answers as they watch. Then check answers as a class. Make sure students understand that the graphs show how often babies hear a certain sound. The frequency of these sounds changes depending on the language being spoken to the child. **Extension:** Have students discuss in small groups about difficulties they have with English sounds. Which sounds are the hardest for them? Are there similar sounds in their native languages or not?

B. Note that students' answers might vary slightly depending on word choice for the second answer. Have students work individually to complete the summary before checking answers as a class.

RECOGNIZING TONE AND MESSAGE

Give students enough time to read the excerpt. Or play the video again to have students listen and read, paying attention to Kuhl's tone as they do. Have students work individually to answer the questions before comparing answers in pairs. For question 2, elicit the words that helped students decide Kuhl's tone. **Extension:** If students did not watch the video again for the exercise, play it again to have students

1. Kuhl is researching babies and their capacity for language learning.; **2.** Answers will vary. Possibilities include: language learning, child development, brain development, education, etc.; **3.** The "critical period" refers to the period, before the age of seven, during which young children are able to acquire different languages easily and quickly.

PART 1

Previewing

The term *rocket science* is a euphemism for something that is extremely complicated and difficult for many to understand.

Getting the Main Ideas

Purpose: sounds

Methodology: changes, time

Results: all, first

Critical Thinking

1. A "culture-bound" listener is one who is only familiar with the sound of his or her own language.; **2.** It may help us become experts in a specific language but hinder our ability to learn a foreign language.

PART 2

Understanding Visuals

A. 1. The graphs show the difference in the /r/ and /l/ sounds produced by English and Japanese speakers.; **2.** Kuhl explains how babies take statistics on the sounds they hear. The graphs show how babies will hear different sounds if they are exposed to different languages and eventually become familiar with the sounds that they hear most often.

B. statistics, culture-bound

Recognizing Tone and Message

1. b; **2.** b, grand and golden age, wondrous, openness

Critical Thinking

1. Answers will vary.; **2.** Both speakers talk about how technology is creating new opportunities for us to go much deeper into certain areas to learn more than we have in the past. In Cox's case, he's talking about space exploration, while Kuhl is talking about the human brain. Both predict that this is only the beginning of a new age of research and exploration in their fields of study.

study Kuhl's body language and intonation, especially in regards to the words students highlighted that show her tone.

CRITICAL THINKING

1. Evaluating. Give students time to think individually before discussing in pairs. Note that students' opinions may differ greatly depending on their own interests as well as learning styles. Some students will find reading a more effective way to take in information while others will prefer listening.

2. Synthesizing. If necessary, let students go back to Unit 1 to review the content about Brian Cox's talk. Elicit ideas about how these two golden ages can be compared in general and what specifically they have in common.

Project | WRITING AND SHARING A BLOG

PROJECT OVERVIEW:

Aims:
- Students research ideas for writing a blog post.
- Students synthesize and analyze what they learned in the unit to explain more about babies and language acquisition and give recommendations to parents.
- Students read and evaluate each other's blog posts and discuss what they learned.

Summary: Students write a blog post about how to best raise bilingual kids. Students use what they learned in the unit to support their research and blog content. The class discusses the blogs, evaluating which advice was the most useful, which ideas were most surprising, etc.

Materials: access to the Internet, word processing software, software or paper for making graphics, printer

Language Support: Agreeing or disagreeing: *I completely agree/disagree.; I agree up to a point, but . . . ; I couldn't agree/disagree more.; I see what you mean, (but) . . .*

TEACHING NOTES

PREPARATION

Give pairs time to look over the list and choose a topic to focus on for their research. Note that students will find varying opinions about each topic online. Tell them to use the research they learned about in the unit as a starting point for their blog content. Tell them they can also choose another aspect of raising bilingual kids other than the topics listed on page 151. Monitor students' choices to make sure that a variety of topics are represented overall. Note the "Language Support" phrases above on the board and review them before students begin the activity.

DURING THE PROJECT

Monitor as pairs work together to write their blog posts. Make sure that both partners are contributing to the research and writing process. Encourage them to make a concept map of the relevant points that they already know from the unit. Then tell them to go online to find any gaps in their information that will help their blog post. Explain that partners should brainstorm together to think of recommendations for parents. Encourage students to support their blogs with visuals to explain the data behind their ideas. Give pairs enough time to write their blogs together. Then hang or pass the blog posts around the classroom for everyone to read. Encourage students to take notes as they read to support the discussion.

AFTER THE PROJECT

After students have read each other's blogs, ask them to evaluate what they learned. What were some of the best suggestions? Did they read any surprising information? Did any of the information contradict research that they read about? What points do they agree with and which do they disagree with? Have each pair share their thoughts about what they learned. *Extension:* Ask students to synthesize everything they learned in the **Project** and write letters to their future selves with tips on how to raise bilingual kids.

EXPLORE MORE

Deb Roy shares how he filmed every moment of his son's first year at home in order to learn more about how babies learn to speak.

A BRIGHTER TOMORROW

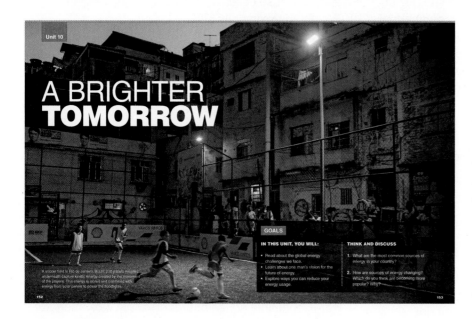

UNIT OVERVIEW

Reading: Students are introduced to challenges we must overcome to transition to renewable energy sources.

TED Talk: Bill Gates talks about the urgent need for new technology to completely eliminate carbon emissions.

Project: Students commit to making one environmentally minded change to their lifestyles for one week.

Lesson 10A PATHS TO THE FUTURE

LESSON OVERVIEW

Aims:
- Read and comprehend an article that explains the difficulties we will face in shifting to renewable resources, and why it's a change that we must make.
- Understand the author's purpose.
- Understand infographics.

Target Vocabulary: alternative, concentrated, diminish, dramatically, emerge, equivalent, ingenuity, intrinsic, require, transition

Reading Passage Summary: Students read about obstacles that we must overcome in order to change our dependency on fossil fuels. There will be challenges, as fossil fuels are easy to access, easy to transport, and rich in power, whereas renewable energy sources are at times inaccessible and also not yet as efficient in producing power. Another issue is the financial cost of this change and how to get people and governments to invest in changes that will save us money in the long term.

TEACHING NOTES

THINK AND DISCUSS

This unit focuses on renewable energy and how we can make the shift to a world that uses sustainable power sources. Use the questions in **Think and Discuss** to review and provide background information on energy in general. For question 1, review what fossil fuels are and how the majority of the world depends on them. Right now, most major electrical plants in the world generate energy using coal, oil, or natural gas. For question 2, elicit students' background knowledge on renewable energy. Have students share what they know to help prepare for the information in the unit ahead.

PRE-READING

A. Give students a minute to look at the pictures and answer question 1. Have them work in pairs to brainstorm ideas for question 2. Then elicit answers and ideas. Write a pro and con list on the board with students' ideas.

Think and Discuss

1. Answers will vary. Most countries in the world still get the majority of their energy from fossil fuels such as coal, oil, and gas. Popular alternative sources of energy include solar power, wind power, geothermal power, and hydropower.; **2.** Answers will vary. The world is becoming more aware of the benefits of choosing renewable sources of energy such as solar power, wind power, geothermal power, and hydropower.

Pre-reading

A. 1. The photo on pages 154–155 shows solar energy production, while page 157 shows coal-powered energy production.; **2.** Answers will vary. Possibilities include:

Fossil Fuels: Pros: easy to obtain, easy to transport, rich in power; **Cons:** not renewable, damage the environment

Renewable Energy: Pros: plentiful, doesn't damage the environment to use; **Cons:** diffused or not concentrated in power

B. ideas and suggestions for a better energy future

Getting the Main Ideas

A. b

B. Paragraphs 1–2: a; **Paragraphs 3–4:** b; **Paragraph 5:** b; **Paragraphs 6–7:** a; **Paragraph 8:** a; **Paragraph 10:** b

Understanding the Author's Purpose

A. Information that students add will vary. See **Answer Key** for Pre-reading.

B. c

Understanding Infographics

A. 1. efficiency, improvements; **2.** a; **3.** a; **4.** b; **5.** b; **6.** improve car fuel efficiency, improve light-truck fuel efficiency, use cellulosic biofuels, car hybridization; **7.** a; **8.** approximately $95

B. 1. reduce/cut/decrease; **2.** save; **3.** invest

Building Vocabulary

A. 1. diminishing; **2.** alternatives; **3.** require; **4.** emerging; **5.** intrinsic

B. 1. c; **2.** d; **3.** b; **4.** e; **5.** a

C. 1. b; **2.** c; **3.** a; **4.** b

Getting Meaning from Context

A. 1. a; **2.** b

B. 1. fossil fuels; **2.** Answers will vary.

Critical Thinking

1. McKibben's tone is serious in paragraph 5. His words contain a sense of urgency: "We've somehow got to . . . we have to do it," etc. Students' reactions will vary.; **2.** His attitude is that if we don't make changes soon and quickly, we will be in a severely precarious situation before we know it. And it is going to take great ingenuity to save us from the coming crisis. Language that he uses to convey this includes: "the toughest thing humans have ever attempted," "we must dramatically change course," "will be catastrophic," etc.

B. Give students one minute to read the introduction and write their answers before discussing in pairs. *Extension:* Have students go online to browse 350.org to learn more about the organization.

DEVELOPING READING SKILLS

GETTING THE MAIN IDEAS

A. Have students read the entire passage, either silently or while listening to the narrated passage on the audio. Have them work individually to complete the activity before checking answers in pairs.

B. Give students a few minutes to go back to the passage to complete the activity before checking answers in pairs. If necessary, go over each statement and its meaning. *Extension:* Have students work in pairs to paraphrase each main message.

UNDERSTANDING THE AUTHOR'S PURPOSE

A. Have students work alone to go back to the passage to find any additional pros and cons. Elicit answers, adding to the pro and con list on the board.

B. Have students work individually to answer the question before checking answers as a class. Note that while McKibben is very clear in his opinion that shifting to renewable energy sources is going to be challenging, he is not without hope. In fact, he offers action steps and even success stories in his article as well. *Extension:* Elicit McKibben's positive news. What action steps and success stories does he also share?

UNDERSTANDING INFOGRAPHICS

A. Give students enough time to carefully read the infographic. Have them work in pairs to answer the questions before checking answers as a class. While the infographic may appear difficult to students at first, the questions in the student book should guide them towards a clearer understanding. Ask students to discuss whether any of the information in the infographic surprised them. If necessary, go over the information in the graphs together to make sure students understand.

B. Have students work individually to complete the summary before checking answers in pairs. Ask pairs to paraphrase the summary in their own words. *Extension:* Ask students to use the data in the infographic to support a written argument about why the U.S. should transition to renewable energy sources.

BUILDING VOCABULARY

A. Have students complete Exercise A individually before checking answers as a class. Something that is *intrinsic* is natural and essential. The verb *diminish* means "to make something grow smaller or decrease." When an amount of something is described as *diminishing*, it can often be inferred that it is getting closer to disappearing entirely.

B. Have students complete Exercise B individually before checking answers as a class. While the passage talks about concentrated energy power, the adjective can be used to describe a range of substances that have a high intensity, especially proportion wise in comparison to something else. For example, concentrated washing detergent only requires a small amount for each wash, or concentrated juice has little or no water added to it.

C. Have students work individually to complete the activity before checking their answers in pairs. Ask pairs to write sentences using each collocation. Elicit examples. *Extension:* Ask students to discuss any examples of energy-related ingenuity that they know. Or have pairs go online to find an example.

GETTING MEANING FROM CONTEXT

A. Give students 30 seconds to work individually to read the examples and choose the definition before checking answers in pairs. Note that *trade-off* usually refers to a compromise made between two choices that are appealing and desirable but incompatible with one another, which is why a compromise must be met. Note that *trade-off* is a key term in the **Project**.

B. Have pairs go over the meaning of each question together. Then have students work individually to write their answers before discussing in pairs. Elicit a class discussion to check answers.

CRITICAL THINKING

Inferring. Give students a few minutes to go back to the two paragraphs referred to in the questions. Ask students to think about attitude, tone, and purpose in both. Encourage students to first decide if he is positive, negative, or neutral, before getting into more specifics about his tone. Note that McKibben's writing has a clear sense of urgency in it. He is saying that whether we adjust or not, the changes are going to come.

EXPLORE MORE

Note that McKibben has a number of articles in *National Geographic*. Students should look for the one titled "Paths to the Future." If time permits, have students also go to 350.org to explore more of McKibben's ideas. Ask them to find out what the number 350 refers to. Encourage students to look into the program *Divest in Fossil Fuels* on McKibben's site and see if it is active in their home countries, and if so, how.

In regards to capitalism, McKibben says that the free market does not offer any negative consequences for those who have high carbon emissions. McKibben believes that if we had a treaty that created a strict limit for carbon emissions, it would impact economic behavior.

LESSON OVERVIEW

Aims:
- Watch and understand a talk by Bill Gates about how technology must help us eliminate our carbon emissions.
- Understand main ideas and key details.
- Summarize information.

TED Talk Summary: In his TED Talk, Bill Gates talks about how we need to get carbon emissions down to zero in the near future. He explains the factors that affect carbon emissions and discusses which ones will make the biggest impact in getting the number to zero. He then explains how we need to develop new technology quickly to make this happen. An annotated transcript for the edited TED Talk is on pages 93–95 of this Teacher's Guide.

TEACHING NOTES

The paragraphs and questions introduce Bill Gates the philanthropist. Explain that the founder of Microsoft and tech guru is also one of the most charitable people on the planet. Like Bono in Unit 5, Gates has used his fame, power, and wealth to make a concentrated effort to change the face of extreme poverty. In this talk, he turns to the topic of energy, explaining in his introduction how it connects back to extreme poverty. Have students work individually to read the paragraphs and answer the questions. Check answers as a class. For question 3, elicit a discussion about how Gates's beliefs might impact his thinking on the energy crisis.

PART 1

PREDICTING

A. Give students a minute to look at the graph and think about the possible positive impacts of falling energy prices. Remind them to consider the group of people that Bill Gates is most trying to help. Have students discuss in pairs before eliciting a class discussion to hear their ideas. If possible, also elicit negative impacts of affordable electricity. *Extension:* Ask students to go online and find energy statistics for their home countries. Tell them to share what they learned with a partner or small group.

B. Have students read over the answer choices. Then play the video. Have students work individually to

complete the sequence before checking answers in pairs. Note that the most extreme result will be at the very end. Have students work individually to complete their answers.

UNDERSTANDING MAIN IDEAS

Have students work individually to write their answers. If necessary, play the video again. Check answers as a class. Encourage a discussion on each of Gates's main ideas. *Extension:* Have students go online to calculate their own carbon footprint. Ask them to describe what they would have to do to reduce it.

CRITICAL THINKING

Analyzing. Note that after listening to only Part 1 of the talk, students will have to both analyze what they've heard and infer conclusions as they think about their answers. Have students first discuss in pairs. Then ask each pair to share their ideas with the class.

PART 2

PREDICTING

Have students work in pairs to predict what each letter might stand for. Explain that each is a key component that affects our carbon emission. Encourage students to use the pictures in the activity and their background knowledge from Lesson A when making their predictions. Ask pairs to share their guesses with the class.

UNDERSTANDING MAIN IDEAS

Play the video. Tell students to check their predictions as they watch. Then have students choose the main idea of this part of Gates's talk.

UNDERSTANDING KEY DETAILS

Have students work individually to complete the chart before checking answers in pairs. Note that the answer options are paraphrases of the key details, not verbatim.

CRITICAL THINKING

Interpreting. Have students discuss their ideas in pairs before eliciting a class discussion. Make sure students understand that Gates does not mean the feat is impossible but instead that a major shift will have to

1. people living in extreme poverty; **2.** HIV/AIDS, agriculture, disaster relief; **3.** They believe in taking on big problems, in finding solutions, and that everyone in the world deserves a healthy, productive life.

PART 1

Predicting

A. Answers will vary. In general, cheaper energy means that more people have access to modern technology in their daily lives, which results in progress and more economic opportunity. Gates says that reduced energy costs create advancements in civilizations.

B. 1. g; **2.** e; **3.** b; **4.** c; **5.** d; **6.** a; **7.** f

Understanding Main Ideas

1. When CO_2 emissions enter the atmosphere, the temperature increases, which in turn creates negative environmental effects such as wild weather and the destruction of ecosystems.

2. No. According to Gates, emissions must be eliminated completely. Even at a very low rate of emissions, there will still be a temperature rise.

Critical Thinking

1. Cutting emissions to zero will reverse the problem of rising temperatures, which will then positively impact the many negative climate changes happening.;
2. Answers will vary.

PART 2

Predicting

Guesses will vary. Actual answers are: Population, Services, Efficiency/Energy, CO_2 per energy unit

Understanding Main Ideas

a

Understanding Key Details

from left to right:
Ways to reduce or limit growth: a, f, b
Problems with reducing or limiting growth: e, d, c

Critical Thinking

Gates means that it's going to take a new technology that creates a giant shift in the way we do things. This new type of technology is going to push us forward, as other new technologies have done in the past.

PART 3

Understanding Key Details

2020: b, e

2050: c, d

Summarizing Information

A. Gates wants the technology that will eliminate carbon emissions to be invented.

B. c

---

happen in the form of the introduction of new technology. *Extension:* Have pairs brainstorm some possible "miracles."

PART 3

UNDERSTANDING KEY DETAILS

Have students look over the chart before watching the video. Then play the video. Have them work individually to complete the chart before checking their answers in pairs. Note that the answers for 2020 appear in the chart in Gates's talk, but he does not actually verbalize the information in his talk (so the information is not in the video script). *Extension:* Ask students to work in pairs or small groups to compare Gates's information and ideas with McKibben's.

SUMMARIZING INFORMATION

A. Give students a minute to read the excerpt. Have them work in pairs. Check answers after students complete Exercise B.

B. Have students work individually to choose the answer. Check answers to Exercises A and B as a class. *Extension:* Ask students to share their thoughts about what Gates says. Do they think it's possible to accomplish what he says?

EXPLORE MORE

TerraPower refers to a developing technology that uses waste from uranium (used in nuclear power plants) to create energy. *Extension:* Have students learn more about efforts to develop sustainable nuclear energy at terrapower.com. Then ask them to share their thoughts on the technology.

PRESENTING A REPORT

PROJECT OVERVIEW:

Aims:
- Students challenge themselves to save energy by changing a daily habit for one week.
- Students write a record of the week in a journal, reflecting on the experience as they do it.
- Students present to others about their experiences, and the class discusses what they learned.

Summary: Students make a change to their lifestyle for a week with the goal of saving energy. They keep a journal to record and reflect on the experience. Students present to the class about their one-week challenge and what they learned. Then students discuss each other's trade-offs.

Materials: paper or computer for journaling, presentation software

Language Support: Reflecting on an experience: *This experience taught me . . . ; It made me think about . . . ; Something else I learned was . . .*

TEACHING NOTES

PREPARATION

Have students work individually. Ask them to look over the list of lifestyle changes in the book. Encourage them to also think of their own ideas. Allow them to do more research online if time permits. Explain that students will commit to doing this activity daily for one week and write about the experience in a journal. Tell them to think about any preparation they may need to do beforehand to make the week successful. For example, if they are giving up meat, they could go to the market to get a supply of vegetables to have at home or make a daily meal plan. Ask students to also read over the questions on page 169 to address in their journal entries. Tell them to record what they do each day as well as their feelings and thoughts about it. Note the "Language Support" phrases on the board and review them before students begin the activity.

DURING THE PROJECT

Tell students to plan a presentation to tell their classmates about their week of making a lifestyle change to save energy. Explain that they should explain the challenge that they set for themselves, talk about the experience, and then offer a concluding thought about what they learned. Ask students to plan a two-minute presentation. Give them time to practice once before presenting to the class. If time permits, have them practice with a partner who then gives them feedback. When students present to the class, tell those who are listening to take notes on their thoughts about what they hear.

AFTER THE PROJECT

Have a class discussion about the presentation and the one-week experience. Ask students to comment on which trade-off seemed the most difficult and which seemed the easiest. Ask students if any habits are ones that they are willing to integrate into their daily lives permanently. ***Extension:*** If students haven't done this in the unit so far, have them go online to calculate their own carbon footprint. Have them think about their own role in energy overuse and what else they can do to change this.

TEDTALK ANNOTATED VIDEO TRANSCRIPTS

BRIAN COX

Why We Need the Explorers

Part 1

We live in difficult and challenging economic times, of course. And one of the first **victims**[1] of difficult economic times, I think, is public spending of any kind, but certainly **in the firing line**[2] at the moment is public spending for science, and particularly curiosity-led science and exploration. So I want to try and convince you in about 15 minutes that that's a ridiculous and ludicrous thing to do.

[. . .] The first thing I want to say, and this is straight from *Wonders of the Solar System*[3], is that our exploration of the solar system and the universe has shown us that it is indescribably beautiful. This is a picture that actually was sent back by the **Cassini space probe**[4] around Saturn, after we'd finished filming *Wonders of the Solar System.* So it isn't in the series. It's of the moon Enceladus. So that big sweeping, white sphere in the corner is Saturn, which is actually in the background of the picture. And that crescent there is the moon Enceladus, which is about as big as the British Isles. It's about 500 kilometers in diameter. So, tiny moon. What's fascinating and beautiful . . . this an unprocessed picture, by the way, I should say, it's black and white, straight from Saturnian orbit.

What's beautiful is, you can probably see on the limb there some faint, sort of, wisps of almost smoke rising up from the limb. This is how we **visualize**[5] that in *Wonders of the Solar System.* It's a beautiful graphic. What we found out were that those faint wisps are actually fountains of ice rising up from the surface of this tiny moon. That's fascinating and beautiful in itself, but we think that the mechanism for powering those fountains requires there to be lakes of liquid water beneath the surface of this moon. And what's important about that is that, on our planet, on Earth, wherever we find liquid water, we find life. So, to find strong evidence of liquid, pools of liquid, beneath the surface of a moon 750 million miles away from the Earth is really quite astounding. So what we're saying, essentially, is maybe that's a habitat for life in the solar system. Well, let me just say, that was a graphic. I just want to show this picture. That's one more picture of Enceladus. This is when Cassini flew beneath Enceladus. So it made a very low pass, just a few hundred kilometers above the surface. And so this, again, a real picture of the ice fountains rising up into space, absolutely beautiful.

[. . .] Our exploration of the solar system has taught us that the solar system is beautiful. It may also have pointed the way to answering one of the most profound questions that you can possibly ask, which is: **"Are we alone in the universe?"**[6] Is there any other use to exploration and science, other than just a sense of wonder? Well, there is. This is a very famous picture taken, actually, on my first

---

[1] Cox uses "victims" here to talk about budget cuts during hard economic times.

[2] Something that is "in the firing line" is being criticized or likely to be gotten rid of. The expression refers to a prisoner being executed by a squad of soldiers firing their guns.

[3] *Wonders of the Solar System* is a TV series that Cox presented.

[4] The Cassini space probe was sent to Saturn in 2004.

[5] By "visualize," Cox is explaining that the image he is showing is a computer graphic made for his TV show.

[6] The question "Are we alone in the universe?" is referring to the existence of alien life forms.

Christmas Eve, December 24th, 1968, when I was about eight months old. It was taken by **Apollo 8**[7] as it went around the back of the moon. **Earthrise**[8] from Apollo 8. A famous picture; many people have said that it's the picture that saved 1968, which was a turbulent year—the student riots in Paris, the height of the Vietnam War. The reason many people think that about this picture, and Al Gore has said it many times, actually, on the stage at TED, is that this picture, arguably, was the beginning of the environmental movement. Because, for the first time, we saw our world, not as a solid, immovable, kind of indestructible place, but as a very small, fragile-looking world just hanging against the blackness of space.

Part 2

What's also not often said about the space exploration, about the Apollo program, is the economic contribution it made. I mean, while you can make arguments that it was wonderful and a tremendous achievement and delivered pictures like this, it cost a lot, didn't it? Well, actually, many studies have been done about the economic effectiveness, the economic impact of Apollo. The biggest one was in 1975 by Chase Econometrics. And it showed that for every $1 spent on Apollo, 14 came back into the U.S. economy. So the Apollo program **paid for itself**[9] in inspiration, in engineering, achievement and, I think, in inspiring young scientists and engineers 14 times over. So exploration can pay for itself.

What about scientific discovery? What about driving innovation? Well, this looks like a picture of virtually nothing. What it is, is a picture of the spectrum of hydrogen. See, back in the 1880s, 1890s, many scientists, many observers, looked at the light given off from atoms. And they saw strange pictures like this. What you're seeing when you put it through a prism is that you heat hydrogen up and it doesn't just glow like a white light, it just emits light at particular colors, a red one, a light blue one, some dark blue ones. Now that led to an understanding of atomic structure because the way that's explained is atoms are a single nucleus with electrons going around them. And the electrons can only be in particular places. And when they jump up to the next place they can be, and fall back down again, they emit light at particular colors.

And so the fact that atoms, when you heat them up, only emit light at very specific colors, was one of the key drivers that led to the development of the **quantum theory**[10], the theory of the structure of atoms.

[. . .] Now, that sounds **esoteric**[11], and indeed it was an esoteric pursuit, but the quantum theory quickly led to an understanding of the behaviors of electrons in materials

---

[7] Apollo 8 was a spacecraft that took three American astronauts into space in 1968. The craft orbited the moon and returned. It was the first to leave Earth's orbit with humans aboard.

[8] "Earthrise" is the name of a photograph taken by an astronaut aboard Apollo 8. The image, which students can see in the video, shows the Earth rising above the moon's horizon.

[9] Something that "pays for itself" creates either a direct or indirect income stream that helps reimburse its cost.

[10] The "quantum theory" explains how molecules move and behave.

[11] Something that is "esoteric" is considered intellectual and often specialized in something that the average person knows nothing about.

like **silicon**[12], for example. The way that silicon behaves, the fact that you can build transistors, is a purely quantum phenomenon. So without that curiosity-driven understanding of the structure of atoms, which led to this rather esoteric theory, quantum mechanics, then we wouldn't have transistors, we wouldn't have silicon chips, we wouldn't have pretty much the basis of our modern economy.

[. . .] This is a beautiful quote that I found—we're talking about **serendipity**[13] there—from **Alexander Fleming**[14]: "When I woke up just after dawn on September 28, 1928, I certainly didn't plan to revolutionize all medicine by discovering the world's first antibiotic." Now, the explorers of the world of the atom did not intend to invent the transistor. And they certainly didn't intend to describe the mechanics of supernova explosions, which eventually told us where the building blocks of life were synthesized in the universe. So, I think science can be— serendipity is important. It can be beautiful. It can reveal quite astonishing things. It can also, I think, finally reveal the most profound ideas to us about our place in the universe and really the value of our home planet.

[. . .] The argument has always been made, and it will always be made, that we know enough about the universe. You could have made it in the 1920s; you wouldn't have had penicillin. You could have made it in the 1890s; you wouldn't have the transistor. And it's made today in these difficult economic times: *Surely, we know enough. We don't need to discover anything else about our universe.*

Let me leave the last words to someone who's rapidly becoming a hero of mine, **Humphrey Davy**[15], who did his science at the turn of the 19th century. He was clearly under assault all the time. "We know enough at the turn of the 19th century. Just exploit it; just build things." He said this, he said, "Nothing is more fatal to the progress of the human mind than to presume that our views of science are ultimate, that our triumphs are complete, that there are no mysteries in nature, and that there are no new worlds to conquer."

This is an edited version of Cox's 2010 TED Talk.
To watch the full talk, visit TED.com.

---

[12] The material "silicon" is used in semi-conductors, which means that modern electronics would not be possible without it.

[13] "Serendipity" is the luck some people have in discovering something valuable by chance.

[14] Alexander Fleming, a scientist from Scotland, invented penicillin by accident. He had gone on an extended holiday and not cleaned up his research area in his laboratory. When he returned, the mold that had formed would lead to his discovery of the first antibiotic for medicine.

[15] Humphrey Davy was a well-known scientist and inventor in England in the 1700s. He was known for his work in electrolysis, as well as the discovery of elements, including calcium.

How to Learn? From Mistakes

Part 1

I have been teaching for a long time, and in doing so have acquired **a body of knowledge**[1] about kids and learning that I really wish more people would understand about the potential of students. In 1931, my grandmother—bottom left for **you guys over here**[2]—graduated from the eighth grade. She went to school to get the information because that's where the information lived. It was in the books; it was inside the teacher's head; and she needed to go there to get the information, because that's how you learned. **Fast-forward**[3] a generation: This is the one-room schoolhouse, Oak Grove, where my father went to a one-room schoolhouse. And he again had to travel to the school to get the information from the teacher, stored it in the only portable memory he has, which is inside his own head, and take it with him, because that is how information was being transported from teacher to student and then used in the world. When I was a kid, we had a set of encyclopedias at my house. It was purchased the year I was born, and it was extraordinary, because I did not have to wait to go to the library to get to the information. The information was inside my house, and it was awesome. This was different than either generation had experienced before, and it changed the way I interacted with information even **at just a small level**[4]. But the information was closer to me. I could get access to it.

[. . .] Fast-forward to Pennsylvania, **where I find myself today**[5]. I teach at the **Science Leadership Academy**[6], which is a partnership school between the Franklin Institute and the school district of Philadelphia. We are a **9 through 12**[7] public school, but we do school quite differently. I moved there primarily to be part of a learning environment that validated the way that I knew that kids learned, and that really wanted to investigate what was possible when you are willing to let go of some of the paradigms of the past, of information scarcity when my grandmother was in school and when my father was in school and even when I was in school, and to a moment when we have information surplus. So what do you do when the information is all around you? Why do you have kids come to school if they no longer have to come there to get the information?

Part 2

In Philadelphia we have **a one-to-one laptop program**[8], so the kids are bringing in laptops with them every day, taking them home, getting access to information. And here's the thing that you need to get comfortable with when you've given the tool to acquire information to students, is that you have to be comfortable with this idea of allowing kids to fail as part of the learning process. We deal right now in the **educational landscape**[9] with an infatuation with the culture of one right

---

[1] Having "a body of" something refers to a large amount of it.

[2] When Laufenberg says "you guys over here," she is addressing her audience directly, to explain where her grandmother is in the picture.

[3] Laufenberg uses the term "fast-forward" a couple of times during her talk to explain the passage of time in her story.

[4] A synonym for "at a small level" is "on a small scale."

[5] When Laufenberg says "where I find myself today," she is referring to her workplace, the school she now works at, and not to the TED conference venue.

[6] Students can find out more about her school at scienceleadershipacademy.org.

[7] The expression "nine through 12" refers to the high school years. The four years of high school in the U.S. are ninth, tenth, 11th, and 12th grades.

[8] A "one-on-one laptop program" means that every student in the school is given a laptop to use by the school.

[9] The noun "landscape" is used here to describe the state of a particular subject. In this case, it's education.

answer that can be **properly bubbled**[10] on the average multiple-choice test, and I am here to share with you: It is not learning. That is the absolute wrong thing to ask, to tell kids to never be wrong. To ask them to always have the right answer doesn't allow them to learn. So we did this project, and this is one of the artifacts of the project. I almost never show them off because of the issue of the idea of failure.

My students produced these infographics as a result of a unit that we decided to do at the end of the year responding to the oil spill. I asked them to take the examples that we were seeing of the infographics that existed in a lot of mass media, and take a look at what were the interesting components of it, and produce one for themselves of a different man-made disaster from American history. And they had certain criteria to do it. They were a little uncomfortable with it, because we'd never done this before, and they didn't know exactly how to do it. They can talk—they're very smooth, and they can write very, very well, but asking them to communicate ideas in a different way was a little uncomfortable for them. But I gave them the room to just do the thing. Go create. Go **figure it out**[11]. Let's see what we can do. And the student that persistently turns out the best visual product did not disappoint. This was done in like two or three days. And this is the work of the student that consistently did it.

And when I sat the students down, I said, "Who's got the best one?" And they immediately went, "There it is." Didn't read anything. "There it is." And I said, "Well, what makes it great?" And they're like, "Oh, the design's good, and he's using good color. And there's some . . ." And they went through all that we processed out loud. And I said, "Go read it." And they're like, "Oh, that one wasn't so awesome." And then we went to another one—it didn't have great visuals, but it had great information—and spent an hour talking about the learning process, because it wasn't about whether or not it was perfect, or whether or not it was what I could create. It asked them to create for themselves, and it allowed them to fail, process, learn from. And when we do another round of this in my class this year, they will do better this time, because learning has to include an amount of failure, because failure is instructional in the process.

[. . .] The main point is that if we continue to look at education as if it's about coming to school to get the information and not about experiential learning, empowering student voice, and embracing failure, we're **missing the mark**[12]. And everything that everybody is talking about today isn't possible if we keep having an educational system that does not value these qualities, because we won't get there with a standardized test, and we won't get there with a culture of one right answer. We know how to do this better, and it's time to do better.

This is an edited version of Laufenberg's 2010 TED Talk. To watch the full talk, visit TED.com.

---

[10] "Properly bubbled" is used here to refer to students guessing the right answer with no real knowledge.

[11] To "figure something out" means to come to understand it or solve it.

[12] To "miss the mark" in a situation means to fail to achieve the intended result.

Why We Have Too Few Women Leaders

Part 1

So for any of us in this room today, let's start out by admitting we're lucky. We don't live in the world our mothers lived in, our grandmothers lived in, where career choices for women were so limited. And if you're in this room today, most of us grew up in a world where we had basic civil rights, and amazingly, we still live in a world where some women don't have them. But **all that aside**[1], we still have a problem, and it's a real problem. And the problem is this: Women are not making it to the top of any profession anywhere in the world. The numbers tell the story quite clearly. 190 heads of state—nine are women. Of all the people in parliament in the world, 13 percent are women. In the corporate sector, women at the top, **C-level jobs**[2], board seats—tops out at 15, 16 percent. The numbers have not moved since 2002 and are going in the wrong direction. And even in the non-profit world, a world we sometimes think of as being led by more women, women at the top: 20 percent.

We also have another problem, which is that women face harder choices between professional success and personal fulfillment. A recent study in the U.S. showed that, of married senior managers, two-thirds of the married men had children and only one-third of the married women had children.

[. . .] So the question is, how are we going to fix this? How do we change these numbers at the top? How do we make this different? I want to start out by saying, I talk about this—about keeping women in the workforce—because I really think that's the answer. In the high-income part of our workforce, in the people who end up at the top—**Fortune 500**[3] CEO jobs, or the equivalent in other industries—the problem, I am convinced, is that women are dropping out. Now people talk about this a lot, and they talk about things like **flextime**[4] and mentoring and programs companies should have to train women. I want to talk about none of that today, even though that's all really important. Today, I want to focus on what we can do as individuals. What are the messages we need to tell ourselves? What are the messages we tell the women who work with and for us? What are the messages we tell our daughters?

Now, at the outset, I want to be very clear that this speech comes with no judgments. I don't have the right answer. I don't even have it for myself. I left San Francisco, where I live, on Monday, and I was getting on the plane for this conference. And my daughter, who's three, when I dropped her off at preschool, did that whole hugging-the-leg, crying, "Mommy, don't get on the plane" thing. This is hard. I feel guilty sometimes. I know no women, whether they're at home or whether they're in the workforce, who don't feel that sometimes. So I'm not saying that staying in the workforce is the right thing for everyone.

My talk today is about what the messages are if you do want to stay in the workforce, and I think there are three. One, sit at the table. Two, make your **partner**[5] a real partner. And three, don't leave before you leave.

[. . .]

---

[1] The expression "all that aside" is used to say that what was previously said is not relevant for what will be said next.

[2] "C-level jobs" refers to those at the head of companies: CEO, CFO, COO, etc. The "C" stands for "Chief."

[3] "Fortune 500" refers to a list of the top 500 companies in the world published yearly by Fortune magazine.

[4] "Flextime" is a system of flexible work hours that some companies offer.

[5] Note that the term "partner" is used by Sandberg here to refer to marriage partner or life partner, not business partner.

Part 2

[W]omen systematically underestimate their own abilities. If you test men and women, and you ask them questions on totally objective criteria like **GPAs**[6], men get it wrong slightly high, and women get it wrong slightly low. Women do not negotiate for themselves in the workforce. A study in the last two years of people entering the workforce out of college showed that 57 percent of boys entering, or men, I guess, are negotiating their first salary, and only seven percent of women. And most importantly, men attribute their success to themselves, and women attribute it to other external factors. If you ask men why they did a good job, they'll say, "I'm awesome. Obviously. Why are you even asking?" If you ask women why they did a good job, what they'll say is someone helped them, they got lucky, they worked really hard. Why does this matter? Boy, it matters a lot because no one gets to **the corner office**[7] by sitting on the side, not at the table, and no one gets the promotion if they don't think they deserve their success, or they don't even understand their own success.

I wish the answer were easy. I wish I could just go tell all the young women I work for, all these fabulous women, "Believe in yourself and negotiate for yourself. **Own your own success**[8]." I wish I could tell that to my daughter. But it's not that simple. Because what the data shows, above all else, is one thing, which is that success and likeability are positively correlated for men and negatively correlated for women. And everyone's nodding, because we all know this to be true.

There's a really good study that shows this really well. There's a famous Harvard Business School study on a woman named Heidi Roizen. And she's an operator in a company in **Silicon Valley**[9], and she uses her contacts to become a very successful **venture capitalist**[10]. In 2002—not so long ago—a professor who was then at Columbia University took that case and made it [Howard] Roizen. And he gave the case out, both of them, to two groups of students. He changed exactly one word: *Heidi* to *Howard*. But that one word made a really big difference. He then surveyed the students, and the good news was the students, both men and women, thought Heidi and Howard were equally competent, and that's good. The bad news was that everyone liked Howard. He's a great guy. You want to work for him. You want to spend the day fishing with him. But Heidi? Not so sure. She's a little **out for herself**[11]. She's a little political. You're not sure you'd want to work for her. This is the complication. We have to tell our daughters and our colleagues, we have to tell ourselves to believe we got the A, to reach for the promotion, to sit at the table, and we have to do it in a world where, for them, there are sacrifices they will make for that, even though for their brothers, there are not.

The saddest thing about all of this is that it's really hard to remember this. And I'm about to tell a story which is truly embarrassing for me, but I think important. I gave this talk at Facebook not so long ago to about 100 employees, and a couple hours later, there was a young woman who works there sitting outside my little desk, and she wanted to talk to

---

[6] "GPA" refers to grade-point average, a score that measures overall educational success in school based on the average grades received in all classes.

[7] The expression "the corner office" refers to a position of success. Traditionally, the head of a company usually has the large corner office with a view.

[8] When you "own something" that you did, it means you take accountability for it and say you are responsible.

[9] Silicon Valley is an area in California where many major technology companies have their offices.

[10] A "venture capitalist" invests in companies, often new ones.

[11] Someone who is "out for themselves" is selfishly motivated.

me. I said, OK, and she sat down, and we talked. And she said, "I learned something today. I learned that I need to keep my hand up." I said, "What do you mean?" She said, "Well, you're giving this talk, and you said you were going to take two more questions. And I had my hand up with lots of other people, and you took two more questions. And I put my hand down, and I noticed all the women put their hand down, and then you took more questions, only from the men." And I thought to myself, wow, if it's me—who cares about this, obviously—giving this talk—and during this talk, I can't even notice that the men's hands are still raised, and the women's hands are still raised, how good are we as managers of our companies and our organizations at seeing that the men are reaching for opportunities more than women? We've got to get women to sit at the table.

[. . .] My generation really, sadly, is not going to change the numbers at the top. They're just not moving. We are not going to get to where 50 percent of the population—in my generation, there will not be 50 percent of [women] at the top of any industry. But I'm hopeful that future generations can. I think a world that was run where half of our countries and half of our companies were run by women, would be a better world. And it's not just because people would know where the women's bathrooms are, even though that would be very helpful. I think it would be a better world. I have two children. I have a five-year-old son and a two-year-old daughter. I want my son to have a choice to contribute fully in the workforce or at home, and I want my daughter to have the choice to not just succeed, but to be liked for her accomplishments.

This is an edited version of Sandberg's 2010 TED Talk. To watch the full talk, visit TED.com.

J.J. ABRAMS

The Mystery Box

Part 1

[. . .] Why do I do so much stuff that involves mystery? And I started trying to figure it out. And I started thinking about why do I do any of what I do, and I started thinking about my grandfather. I loved my grandfather. Harry Kelvin was his name, my mother's father. He died in 1986. He was an amazing guy. And one of the reasons he was amazing: After World War II, he began an electronics company. He started selling surplus parts, kits, to schools and stuff. So he had this incredible curiosity. As a kid, I saw him come over to me with radios and telephones and all sorts of things. And he'd open them up, he'd unscrew them, and reveal the inner workings—which many of us, I'm sure, **take for granted**[1]. But it's an amazing gift to give a kid. To open up this thing and show how it works and why it works and what it is. He was the ultimate deconstructor, in many ways.

[. . .] He sort of **humored**[2] my obsession to other things, too, like magic. The thing is, we'd go to this magic store in New York City called Lou Tannen's Magic. It was this great magic store. It was a **crappy**[3] little building in **Midtown**[4], but you'd be in the elevator, the elevator would open—there'd be this little, small magic store. You'd be in the magic store. And it was just, it was a magical place. So I got all these sort of magic tricks. Oh, here. I'll show you. This is the kind of thing. So it would be like, you know. Right? Which is good, but now I can't move. Now, I have to do this, the rest of the thing, like this. I'm like, "Oh, wow. Look at my computer over there!"

Anyway, so one of the things that I bought at the magic store was this: Tannen's Mystery Magic Box. The **premise**[5] behind the mystery magic box was the following: 15 dollars buys you 50 dollars worth of magic. Which is a savings. Now, I bought this decades ago and I'm not kidding. If you look at this, you'll see it's never been opened. But I've had this forever. Now, I was looking at this, it was in my office, as it always is, on the shelf, and I was thinking, why have I not opened this? And why have I kept it? Because I'm not a **pack rat**[6]. I don't keep everything, but for some reason I haven't opened this box. And I felt like there was a key to this, somehow, in talking about something at TED that I haven't discussed before, and bored people elsewhere. So I thought, maybe there's something with this. I started thinking about it. And there was this giant question mark. I love the design, for what it's worth, of this thing. And I started thinking, why haven't I opened it? And I realized that I haven't opened it because it represents something important—to me. It represents my grandfather. Am I allowed to cry at TED? Because—no, I'm not going to cry. But—the thing is, that it represents infinite possibility. It represents hope. It represents potential. And what I love about this box, and what I realize I sort of do in whatever it is that I do, is I find myself drawn to infinite possibility, that sense of potential. And I realize that mystery is the catalyst for imagination. Now, it's not the most **groundbreaking**[7] idea, but when I started to think that maybe there are times when mystery is more important than knowledge, I started getting interested in this.

---

[1] When we "take something for granted" we don't fully appreciate it.

[2] To "humor" someone means to go along with what someone wants even if you don't agree.

[3] The adjective "crappy" is a colloquial term used to describe something of poor quality.

[4] "Midtown" refers to an area of Manhattan in New York City.

[5] A "premise" is a fundamental idea that shapes something.

[6] A "pack rat" is a person who saves everything, including things that are no longer useful.

[7] Something that is "groundbreaking" is innovative and new.

[. . .] What's a bigger mystery box than a movie theater? You know? You go to the theater, you're just so excited to see anything. The moment the lights go down is often the best part, you know? And you're full of that amazing—that feeling of excited anticipation. And often, the movie's, like, there and it's going, and then something happens and you go, "Oh—" and then something else, and you're, "Mmm . . ." Now, when it's a great movie, you're along for the ride 'cause you're willing to give yourself to it.

Part 2

[. . .] This is something online; I don't know if you've seen it before. Six years ago, they did this. This is an online thing done by guys who had some visual effects experience. But the point was that they were doing things that were using these mystery boxes that they had—everyone has now. What I've realized is what my grandfather did for me when I was a kid, everyone has access to now. You don't need to have my grandfather, though you wished you had. But I have to tell you—this is a guy doing stuff on a **Quadra 950 computer**[8]— the resolution's a little bit low—using **Infinity software**[9] they stopped making 15 years ago. He's doing stuff that looks as amazing as stuff I've seen released from Hollywood.

The most incredible sort of mystery, I think, is now the question of what comes next. Because it is now **democratized**[10]. So now, the creation of media is—it's everywhere. The stuff that I was lucky and begging for to get when I was a kid is now ubiquitous. And so, there's an amazing sense of opportunity out there. And when I think of the filmmakers who exist out there now who would have been silenced, you know—who have been silenced in the past—it's a very exciting thing.

I used to say in classes and lectures and stuff, to someone who wants to write, "Go! Write! Do your thing." It's free, you know, you don't need permission to go write. But now I can say, "Go make your movie!" There's nothing stopping you from going out there and getting the technology. You can lease, rent, buy stuff off the shelf that is either as good, or just as good, as the stuff that's being used by the, you know, **quote unquote**[11] "legit people." No community is best served when only the elite have control. And I feel like this is an amazing opportunity to see what else is out there.

Part 3

When I did *Mission: Impossible III*, we had amazing visual effects stuff. **ILM**[12] did the effects; it was incredible. And sort of like my dream to be involved. And there are a couple of sequences in the movie, like these couple of moments I'll show you. There's that.

OK, obviously I have an obsession with big crazy explosions. So my favorite visual effect in the movie is the one I'm about to show you. And it's a scene in which **Tom's**[13] character wakes up. He's drowsy. He's crazy—out of it. And the guy wakes up, and he shoves this gun in his nose and shoots this little capsule into his brain that he's going to use later to kill him, as bad guys do.

---

[8] The "Quadra 950 computer" refers to an early Apple computer that was discontinued in the mid-1990s.

[9] "Infinity software" refers to an outdated software program.

[10] Something that is "democratized" is available to everyone.

[11] The expression "quote unquote" is a spoken phrase which refers to putting quotation marks before and after the next word that you say. This is usually done to indicate that the words are not something that the speaker would agree with.

[12] ILM is the special effects company, Industrial Light & Magic.

[13] Abrams is referring to actor Tom Cruise who starred in *Mission: Impossible III.*

Bad Guy: Good morning.

OK, now. When we shot that scene, we were there doing it, the actor who had the gun, an English actor, Eddie Marsan— sweetheart, great guy—he kept taking the gun and putting it into Tom's nose, and it was hurting Tom's nose. And I learned this very early on in my career: Don't hurt Tom's nose. There are three things you don't want to do. Number two is: Don't hurt Tom's nose. So Eddie has this gun—and he's the greatest guy—he's this really sweet English guy. He's like, "Sorry, I don't want to hurt you." I'm like—you gotta—we have to make this look good. And I realized that we had to do something 'cause it wasn't working just as it was. And I literally, like, thought back to what I would have done using the **Super 8 camera**[14] that my grandfather got me sitting in

that room, and I realized that hand didn't have to be Eddie Marsan's. It could be Tom's. And Tom would know just how hard to push the gun. He wouldn't hurt himself.

So we took his hand and we painted it to look a little bit more like Eddie's. We put it in Eddie's sleeve, and so the hand that you see—I'll show you again, that's not Eddie's hand, that's Tom's. So Tom is playing two roles. And he didn't ask for any more money. So here, here. Watch it again. There he is. He's waking up. He's drowsy, been through a lot. Tom's hand. Tom's hand. Tom's hand. Anyway. So. Thanks. So you don't need the greatest technology to do things that can work in movies. And the mystery box, in honor of my grandfather, stays closed. Thank you.

This is an edited version of Abrams' 2007 TED Talk.
To watch the full talk, visit TED.com.

---

[14] The "Super 8 camera" was a popular home motion picture camera in the 1960s and 1970s using 8mm format. Abrams wrote and directed a film called *Super 8*.

The Good News on Poverty (Yes, There's Good News)

Part 1

[. . .] So I thought, forget the rock opera, forget the bombast, my usual tricks. The only thing singing today would be the facts, for I have truly embraced my inner nerd.

So exit the rock star. Enter the evidence-based activist, the factivist.

Because what the facts are telling us is that the long, slow journey, humanity's long, slow journey of equality, is actually speeding up. Look at what's been achieved. Look at the pictures these data sets print. Since the year 2000, since the turn of the millennium, there are eight million more AIDS patients getting life-saving antiretroviral drugs. Malaria: There are eight countries in sub-Saharan Africa that have their death rates cut by 75 percent. For kids under five, child mortality, kids under five, it's down by 2.65 million a year. That's a rate of 7,256 children's lives saved each day. Wow. Wow.

Let's just stop for a second, actually, and think about that. Have you read anything anywhere in the last week that is remotely as important as that number? Wow. Great news. It drives me nuts that most people don't seem to know this news. Seven thousand kids a day. Here's two of them. This is Michael and Benedicta, and they're alive thanks in large part to **Dr. Patricia Asamoah**[1]—she's amazing—and **the Global Fund**[2], which all of you financially support, whether you know it or not. And the Global Fund provides antiretroviral drugs that stop mothers from passing HIV to their kids. This fantastic news didn't happen by itself. It was fought for, it was campaigned for, it was innovated for. And this great news gives birth to even more great news, because the historic trend is this. The number of people living in back-breaking, **soul-crushing**[3] extreme poverty has declined from 43 percent of the world's population in 1990 to 33 percent by 2000 and then to 21 percent by 2010. **Give it up**[4] for that. Halved. Halved.

Now, the rate is still too high—still too many people unnecessarily losing their lives. There's still work to do. But it's heart-stopping. It's **mind-blowing**[5] stuff. And if you live on less than $1.25 a day, if you live in that kind of poverty, this is not just data. This is everything. If you're a parent who wants the best for your kids—and I am—this rapid transition is a route out of despair and into hope. And guess what! If the trajectory continues, look where the amount of people living on $1.25 a day gets to by 2030. Can't be true, can it? That's what the data is telling us. If the trajectory continues, we get to, wow, the zero zone.

[. . .]

Part 2

So why aren't we jumping up and down about this? Well, the opportunity is real, but so is the jeopardy. We can't get this done until we really accept that we can get this done. Look at

---

[1] Dr. Patricia Nkansah-Asamoah is a Ghanaian doctor and activist known for her work with HIV-positive mothers in Accra. She is involved with Bono's organization ONE.

[2] The Global Fund invests millions of dollars every year in programs that aim to solve problems caused by malaria, tuberculosis, and AIDS. Learn more at globalfund.org.

[3] Something that is "soul-crushing" makes you feel that there is no hope.

[4] The expression "give it up" is used to encourage an audience to applaud.

[5] Something that is "mind-blowing" is amazing.

this graph. It's called inertia. It's how we **screw it up[6]**. And the next one is really beautiful. It's called momentum. And it's how we can **bend the arc of history[7]** down towards zero, just doing the things that we know work.

So inertia versus momentum. There is jeopardy, and of course, the closer you get, it gets harder. We know the obstacles that are in our way right now, in difficult times. In fact, today in your capital, in difficult times, **some who mind the nation's purse[8]** want to cut life-saving programs like the Global Fund. But you can do something about that. You can tell politicians that these cuts [can cost] lives.

Right now today, in Oslo as it happens, oil companies are fighting to keep secret their payments to governments for extracting oil in developing countries. You can do something about that, too. You can join the One Campaign, and leaders like **Mo Ibrahim[9]**, the telecom entrepreneur. We're pushing for laws that make sure that at least some of the wealth under the ground ends up in the hands of the people living above it.

And right now, we know that the biggest disease of all is not a disease. It's corruption. But there's a vaccine for that, too. It's called transparency, open data sets, something the TED community is really on it. Daylight, you could call it, transparency. And technology is really **turbocharging[10]** this. It's getting harder to hide if you're doing bad stuff.

So let me tell you about the U-report, which I'm really excited about. It's 150,000 **millennials[11]** all across Uganda, young people armed with 2G phones, an SMS social network exposing government corruption and demanding to know what's in the budget and how their money is being spent. This is exciting stuff.

Look, once you have these tools, you can't not use them. Once you have this knowledge, you can't un-know it. You can't delete this data from your brain, but you can delete the clichéd image of supplicant, impoverished peoples not taking control of their own lives. You can erase that, you really can, because it's not true anymore.

It's transformational. 2030? By 2030, robots, not just serving us Guinness, but drinking it. By the time we get there, every place with a rough semblance of governance might actually be on their way.

So I'm here to—I guess we're here to try and infect you with this virtuous, data-based virus, the one we call factivism. It's not going to kill you. In fact, it could save countless lives. I guess we in the One Campaign would love you to be contagious, spread it, share it, pass it on. By doing so, you will join us and countless others in what I truly believe is the greatest adventure ever taken, the ever-demanding journey of equality.

[. . .]

This is an edited version of Bono's 2013 TED Talk.
To watch the full talk, visit TED.com.

---

[6] To "screw something up" means to ruin the chance for success.

[7] An event or happening that "bends the arc of history," has a far-reaching effect that changes the course of the human race.

[8] To "mind a purse" means to be in control of the money. In this case, Bono is referring to federal budgets.

[9] Mo Ibrahim gained financial success as a telecom entrepreneur, and then set up the Mo Ibrahim Foundation to encourage more responsibility in governments in Africa.

[10] A synonym for "turbocharge" is "accelerate."

[11] The term "millennials" is usually considered to apply to individuals who reached adulthood around the turn of the 21st century.

Ancient Wonders Captured in 3-D

Part 1

I'd like to start with a short story. It's about a little boy whose father was a history buff and who used to **take him by the hand**[1] to visit the ruins of an ancient metropolis on the outskirts of their camp. They would always stop by to visit these huge winged bulls that used to guard the gates of that ancient metropolis, and the boy used to be scared of these winged bulls, but at the same time they excited him. And the dad used to use those bulls to tell the boy stories about that civilization and their work.

Let's **fast-forward**[2] to the San Francisco Bay Area many decades later, where I started a technology company that brought the world its first 3D laser scanning system. Let me show you how it works.

[Video] *Female Voice: Long-range laser scanning works by sending out a pulse that's a laser beam of light. The system measures the beam's time of flight, recording the time it takes for the light to hit a surface and make its return. With two mirrors, the scanner calculates the beam's horizontal and vertical angles, giving accurate x, y, and z coordinates. The point is then recorded into a 3D visualization program. All of this happens in seconds.*

You can see here, these systems are extremely fast. They collect millions of points at a time with very high accuracy and very high resolution. A **surveyor**[3] with traditional survey tools would **be hard-pressed to**[4] produce maybe 500 points in a whole day. These **babies**[5] would be producing something like ten thousand points a second. So, as you can imagine, this was **a paradigm shift**[6] in the survey and construction as well as in reality-capture industry.

Approximately ten years ago, my wife and I started a foundation to do good, and right about that time, the magnificent Bamiyan Buddhas, hundred and eighty foot tall in Afghanistan, were blown up by the Taliban. They were gone in an instant. And unfortunately, there was no detailed documentation of these Buddhas. This clearly devastated me, and I couldn't help but wonder about the fate of my old friends, the winged bulls, and the fate of the many, many heritage sites all over the world. Both my wife and I were so touched by this that we decided to expand the mission of our foundation to include digital heritage preservation of world sites. We called the project CyArk, which stands for Cyber Archive.

Part 2

To date[7], with the help of a global network of partners, we've completed close to fifty projects. Let me show you some of them: Chichen Itza, Rapa Nui—and what you're seeing here are the cloud of points—Babylon, Rosslyn Chapel, Pompeii, and our latest project, Mt. Rushmore, which happened to be one of our most challenging projects. As you see here, we had to develop a special rig to bring the scanner up close and personal. The results of our work in the field are used to

---

[1] When you "take someone by the hand" you hold their hand and lead them.

[2] Students also heard TED speaker Diana Laufenberg use the term "fast-forward" to move a story ahead in Unit 2.

[3] A "surveyor" has the job of measuring three-dimensional points between distances. It is a common job in the construction industry.

[4] When someone "is hard-pressed" to do something, that person is going to face difficulties accomplishing it, likely because of not having enough time or money.

[5] The term "baby" is used colloquially sometimes to refer to machines, especially impressive ones.

[6] A "paradigm shift" completely changes the way something has been done up until that point.

[7] The phrase "to date" means "up until the present time."

produce media and **deliverables**[8] to be used by conservators and researchers. We also produce media for dissemination to the public—free through the CyArk website. These would be used for education, cultural tourism, etc.

What you're looking at in here is a 3D viewer that we developed that would allow the display and manipulation of [the] cloud of points in real time, cutting sections through them and extracting dimensions. This happens to be the cloud of points for **Tikal**[9]. In here you see a traditional 2D architectural engineering drawing that's used for preservation, and of course we tell the stories through fly-throughs. And here, this is a **fly-through**[10] the cloud of points of Tikal, and here you see it rendered and photo-textured with the photography that we take of the site. And so this is not a video. This is actual 3D points with two- to three-millimeter accuracy. And of course the data can be used to develop 3D models that are very accurate and very detailed. And here you're looking at a model that's extracted from the cloud of points for Stirling Castle. It's used for studies, for visualization, as well as for education.

And finally, we produce mobile apps that include narrated virtual tools. The more I got involved in the heritage field, the more it became clear to me that we are losing the sites and the stories faster than we can physically preserve them. Of course, earthquakes and all the natural phenomena—floods, tornadoes, etc.—**take their toll**[11]. However, what occurred to me was human-caused destruction, which was not only causing a significant portion of the destruction, but actually it was accelerating. This includes arson, urban sprawl, acid rain, not to mention terrorism and wars. It was getting more and more apparent that we're **fighting a losing battle**[12]. We're losing our sites and the stories, and basically we're losing a piece—and a significant piece—of our collective memory. Imagine us as a human race not knowing where we came from.

[. . .] Let me close with another short story. Two years ago, we were approached by a partner of ours to digitally preserve an important heritage site, a UNESCO heritage site in Uganda, the Royal Kasubi Tombs. The work was done successfully in the field, and the data was archived and publicly disseminated through the CyArk website. Last March, we received very sad news. The Royal Tombs had been destroyed by suspected arson. A few days later, we received a call: "Is the data available and can it be used for reconstruction?" Our answer, of course, was yes.

Let me leave you with a final thought. Our heritage is much more than our collective memory—it's our collective treasure. We owe it to our children, our grandchildren, and the generations we will never meet to keep it safe and to pass it along. Thank you.

This is an edited version of Kacyra's 2011 TED Talk.
To watch the full talk, visit TED.com.

---

[8] A "deliverable" is a general term used to describe a product to be provided.

[9] Tikal is a Mayan ruin in Guatemala.

[10] A "fly-through" usually refers to a computer simulated experience that lets you view a site from above, as though you are flying through it.

[11] When something "takes its toll," it means that it creates a negative impact.

[12] The expression "fighting a losing battle" is used when it seems that success is impossible because the obstacles to overcome are too strong or too many.

How Food Shapes Our Cities

Part 1

How do you feed a city? It's one of the great questions of our time. Yet it's one that's rarely asked. We **take it for granted[1]** that if we go into a shop or restaurant, or indeed into this theater's foyer in about an hour's time, there is going to be food there waiting for us, having magically come from somewhere.

But when you think that every day for a city the size of London, enough food has to be produced, transported, bought and sold, cooked, eaten, disposed of, and that something similar has to happen every day for every city on Earth, it's remarkable that cities get fed at all.

We live in places like this as if they're the most natural things in the world, forgetting that because we're animals and that we need to eat, we're actually as dependent on the natural world as our ancient ancestors were. And as more of us move into cities, more of that natural world is being transformed into extraordinary landscapes like the one behind me—it's soybean fields in Mato Grosso in Brazil—in order to feed us. These are extraordinary landscapes, but few of us ever get to see them.

And increasingly, these landscapes are not just feeding us either. As more of us move into cities, more of us are eating meat, so that a third of the annual grain crop globally now gets fed to animals rather than to us human animals. And given that it takes three times as much grain—**actually ten times as much grain[2]**—to feed a human if it's passed through an animal first, that's not a very efficient way of feeding us.

And it's **an escalating problem[3]**, too. By 2050, it's estimated that twice the number of us are going to be living in cities. And it's also estimated that there is going to be twice as much meat and dairy consumed. So meat and urbanism are rising hand in hand. And that's going to pose an enormous problem. Six billion hungry carnivores to feed, by 2050. That's a big problem. And actually if we carry on as we are, it's a problem we're very unlikely to be able to solve.

Nineteen million hectares of rain forest are lost every year to create new arable land. Although at the same time we're losing an equivalent amount of existing arables to **salinization[4]** and erosion. We're very hungry for fossil fuels, too. It takes about 10 calories to produce every calorie of food that we consume in the West. And even though there is food that we are producing at great cost, we don't actually value it. Half the food produced in the U.S.A. is currently thrown away. And to end all of this, at the end of this long process, we're not even managing to feed the planet properly. A billion of us are obese, while a further billion starve. None of it makes very much sense.

And when you think that 80 percent of global trade in food now is controlled by just five multinational corporations, it's **a grim picture[5]**. As we're moving into cities, the world is also embracing a Western diet. And if we look to the future, it's an unsustainable diet. [. . .]

Part 2

Here we have food—that used to be the center, the social core of the city—at the periphery. It used to be a social event, buying and selling food. Now it's anonymous. We used to cook; now we just add water, or a little bit of an egg if you're making a cake or something. We don't smell food to see if it's OK to eat. We just read the back of a label on a packet. And we don't value food. We don't trust it. So instead of trusting it, we fear it. And instead of valuing it, we throw it away.

One of the great ironies of modern food systems is that they've made the very thing they promised to make easier much harder. By making it possible to build cities anywhere and any place, they've actually distanced us from our most important relationship, which is that of us and nature. And also they've made us dependent on systems that only they can deliver, that, as we've seen, are unsustainable.

So what are we going to do about that? It's not a new question. 500 years ago, it's what Thomas More was asking himself. This is the frontispiece of his book **_Utopia_[6]**. And it

---

[1] When we "take something for granted," we don't appreciate it at the time. J.J. Abrams also used this expression in his TED talk.

[2] Students should note that Steel corrects her statistic here. She first mistakenly says "three times."

[3] An "escalating problem" is one that is getting worse and worse.

[4] The process of salinization involves putting salt into something, usually water.

[5] A "grim picture" is a very negative situation.

[6] Thomas Moore's book _Utopia_ was the first time the word "utopia" was used. It is now a common word for talking about an ideal place.

was a series of semi-independent city-states, if that sounds remotely familiar, a day's walk from one another where everyone was basically farming-mad, and grew vegetables in their back gardens, and ate communal meals together, and so on. And I think you could argue that food is a fundamental ordering principle of Utopia, even though More never framed it that way.

[. . .] *Utopia* was actually a word that Thomas More used deliberately. It was a kind of joke, because it's got a double derivation from the Greek. It can either mean a good place, or no place. Because it's an ideal. It's an imaginary thing. We can't have it. And I think, as a conceptual tool for thinking about the very deep problem of human dwelling, that makes it not much use. So I've come up with an alternative, which is *Sitopia*, from the ancient Greek, "sitos" for food, and "topos" for place.

I believe we already live in Sitopia. We live in a world shaped by food, and if we realize that, we can use food as a really powerful tool—a conceptual tool, design tool, to shape the world differently. So if we were to do that, what might Sitopia look like? Well, I think it looks a bit like this. I have to use this slide. It's just the look on the face of the dog. But anyway, this is—it's food at the center of life, at the center of family life, being celebrated, being enjoyed, people taking time for it. This is where food should be in our society.

But you can't have scenes like this unless you have people like this. By the way, these can be men as well. It's people who think about food, who think ahead, who plan, who can stare at a pile of raw vegetables and actually recognize them. We need these people. We're part of a network. Because without these kinds of people, we can't have places like this. Here, I deliberately chose this because it is a man buying a vegetable. But networks, markets where food is being grown locally. It's common. It's fresh. It's part of the social life of the city. Because without that, you can't have this kind of place, food that is grown locally and also is part of the landscape,

and is not just **a zero-sum commodity**[7] off in some unseen **hell-hole**[8]. Cows with a view. Steaming piles of humus. This is basically bringing the whole thing together.

And this is a community project I visited recently in Toronto. It's a greenhouse, where kids get told all about food and growing their own food. Here is a plant called Kevin, or maybe it's a plant belonging to a kid called Kevin. I don't know. But anyway, these kinds of projects that are trying to reconnect us with nature is extremely important.

So Sitopia, for me, is really a way of seeing. It's basically recognizing that Sitopia already exists in **little pockets**[9] everywhere. The trick is to join them up, to use food as a way of seeing. And if we do that, we're going to stop seeing cities as big, metropolitan, unproductive blobs, like this. We're going to see them more like this, as part of the productive, organic framework of which they are inevitably a part, symbiotically connected. But of course, that's not a great image either, because we need not to be producing food like this anymore. We need to be thinking more about permaculture, which is why I think this image just sums up for me the kind of thinking we need to be doing. It's a re-conceptualization of the way food shapes our lives.

The best image I know of this is from 650 years ago. It's **Ambrogio Lorenzetti's**[10] "Allegory of Good Government." It's about the relationship between the city and the countryside. And I think the message of this is very clear. If the city looks after the country, the country will look after the city. And I want us to ask now, what would Ambrogio Lorenzetti paint if he painted this image today? What would an allegory of good government look like today? Because I think it's an urgent question. It's one we have to ask and we have to start answering. We know we are what we eat. We need to realize that the world is also what we eat. But if we take that idea, we can use food as a really powerful tool to shape the world better. Thank you very much.

This is an edited version of Steel's 2009 TED Talk.
To watch the full talk, visit TED.com.

---

[7] Something that is a "zero-sum commodity" is one that one group gains while another one loses. Steel believes modern food production makes food a zero-sum commodity that humans gain from while the planet's environment loses.

[8] A "hell-hole" is a terrible place.

[9] The term "little pockets" is used here to describe small areas where certain things are happening.

[10] Ambrogio Lorenzetti was an Italian painter who lived in the 1300s.

What Will Future Jobs Look Like?

Part 1

The writer **George Eliot**[1] cautioned us that, among all forms of mistake, prophesy is the most gratuitous. The person that we would all acknowledge as her 20th-century counterpart, **Yogi Berra**[2], agreed. He said, "It's tough to make predictions, especially about the future."

I'm going to ignore their cautions and make one very specific forecast. In the world that we are creating very quickly, we're going to see more and more things that look like science fiction, and fewer and fewer things that look like jobs. Our cars are very quickly going to start driving themselves, which means we're going to need fewer truck drivers. We're going to hook Siri up to Watson and use that to automate a lot of the work that's currently done by customer service reps and troubleshooters and diagnosers, and we're already taking **R2D2**[3], painting him orange, and putting him to work carrying shelves around warehouses, which means we need a lot fewer people to be walking up and down those aisles.

Now, for about 200 years, people have been saying exactly what I'm telling you—the age of technological unemployment is at hand—starting with the Luddites smashing looms in Britain just about two centuries ago, and they have been wrong. Our economies in the developed world have **coasted along**[4] on something pretty close to full employment.

Which brings up a critical question: Why is this time different, if it really is? The reason it's different is that, just in the past few years, our machines have started demonstrating skills they have never, ever had before: understanding, speaking, hearing, seeing, answering, writing, and they're still acquiring new skills. For example, mobile humanoid robots are still incredibly primitive, but the **research arm**[5] of the Defense Department just launched a competition to have them do things like this, and if the track record is any guide, this competition is going to be successful. So when I look around, I think the day is not too far off at all when we're going to have androids doing a lot of the work that we are doing right now. And we're creating a world where there is going to be more and more technology and fewer and fewer jobs. It's a world that **Erik Brynjolfsson**[6] and I are calling "the new machine age." The thing to keep in mind is that this is absolutely great news.

Part 2

[. . .] We are seeing an amazing flourishing taking place. In a world where it is just about as easy to generate an object as it is to print a document, we have amazing new possibilities.

The people who used to be craftsmen and hobbyists are now makers, and they're responsible for massive amounts of innovation. And artists who were formerly constrained can now do things that were never, ever possible for them before. So this is a time of great flourishing, and the more I look around, the more convinced I become that this quote, from the physicist Freeman Dyson, is not **hyperbole**[7] at all. This is just a plain statement of the facts. We are in the middle of an astonishing period.

"Technology is a gift of God. After the gift of life it is perhaps the greatest of God's gifts. It is the mother of civilizations, of arts and of sciences." — Freeman Dyson

Which brings up another great question: What could possibly go wrong in this new machine age, right?

[. . .]

---

[1] George Eliot was an English writer in the 1800s. Eliot wrote under a pen name. Her real name was Mary Ann Evans.

[2] Yogi Berra is a popular American sports figure who played catcher, as well as worked as coach and manager, for the New York Yankees baseball team.

[3] "R2D2" refers to a robot character that appears in the Star Wars movie series.

[4] Something that "coasts along" continues at a steady speed.

[5] The noun "arm" can be used to describe a division in a company or organization.

[6] Erik Brynjolfsson is a professor of Internet Technology Productivity at MIT.

[7] The noun "hyperbole" is used to describe a statement that is exaggerated.

Part 3

To tell you the kinds of societal challenges that are going to come up in the new machine age, I want to tell a story about two stereotypical American workers. And to make them really stereotypical, let's make them both white guys. And the first one is a college-educated professional, creative type, manager, engineer, doctor, lawyer, that kind of worker. We're going to call him "Ted." He's at the top of the American middle class. His counterpart is not college-educated and works as a laborer, works as a clerk, does low-level **white collar**[8] or **blue collar**[9] work in the economy. We're going to call that guy "Bill."

And if you go back about 50 years, Bill and Ted were leading remarkably similar lives. For example, in 1960 they were both very likely to have full-time jobs, working at least 40 hours a week. But as the social researcher **Charles Murray**[10] has documented, as we started to automate the economy, and 1960 is just about when computers started to be used by businesses, as we started to progressively inject technology and automation and digital stuff into the economy, the fortunes of Bill and Ted diverged a lot. Over this time frame, Ted has continued to hold a full-time job. Bill hasn't. In many cases, Bill has left the economy entirely, and Ted very rarely has. Over time, Ted's marriage has stayed quite happy. Bill's hasn't. And Ted's kids have grown up in a two-parent home, while Bill's absolutely have not over time. Other ways that Bill is dropping out of society? He's decreased his voting in presidential elections, and he's started to go to prison a lot more often. So I cannot tell a happy story about these social trends, and they don't show any signs of reversing themselves. They're also true no matter which ethnic group or demographic group we look at, and they're actually getting so severe that they're in danger of overwhelming even the amazing progress we made with the Civil Rights Movement.

And what my friends in Silicon Valley and Cambridge are overlooking is that they're Ted. They're living these amazingly busy, productive lives, and they've got all the benefits to show from that, while Bill is leading a very different life. They're actually both proof of how right Voltaire was when he talked about the benefits of work, and the fact that it saves us from not one but three great evils. *"Work saves a man from three great evils: boredom, vice, and need."* — Voltaire

Part 4

[W]ith these challenges, what do we do about them?

The **economic playbook**[11] is surprisingly clear, surprisingly straightforward, in the short term especially. The robots are not going to take all of our jobs in the next year or two, so the classic **Econ 101**[12] playbook is going to work just fine: Encourage entrepreneurship, **double down on**[13] infrastructure, and make sure we're turning out people from our educational system with the appropriate skills.

But over the longer term, if we are moving into an economy that's heavy on technology and light on labor, and we are, then we have to consider some more radical interventions, for example, something like a guaranteed minimum income. [. . .] And if you find yourself worried that something like a guaranteed income is going to stifle our drive to succeed and make us kind of complacent, you might be interested to know that social mobility, one of the things we really pride ourselves on in the United States, is now lower than it is in the northern European countries that have these very generous **social safety nets**[14]. So the economic playbook is actually pretty straightforward.

The societal one is a lot more challenging. I don't know what the playbook is for getting Bill to engage and stay engaged throughout life.

---

[8] "Low-level white collar" work refers to jobs in offices that require a low skill level, such as photocopying.

[9] "Blue collar" work refers to manual, physical labor.

[10] Charles Murray has written extensively on social policy in the U.S.

[11] A "playbook" refers to a book with tactics and strategies written in it, usually used for sports. McAfee uses the term as a synonym for "strategy."

[12] "Econ 101" refers to the basic economics class that all college and university students take to learn the fundamentals of economics.

[13] The term "double down" is a gambling term used when doubling a bet. McAfee is saying we have to invest much more in infrastructure.

[14] A "social safety net" refers to public programs in place that help people in difficult financial situations.

I do know that education is a huge part of it. I witnessed this firsthand. I was a Montessori kid for the first few years of my education, and what that education taught me is that the world is an interesting place and my job is to go explore it. The school stopped in third grade, so then I entered the public school system, and it felt like I had been sent to the **Gulag**[15]. With the benefit of hindsight, I now know the job was to prepare me for life as a clerk or a laborer, but at the time it felt like the job was to kind of bore me into some submission with what was going on around me. We have to do better than this. We cannot keep turning out Bills.

[. . .] I started my talk with quotes from wordsmiths who were separated by an ocean and a century. Let me end it with words from politicians who were similarly distant.

Winston Churchill came to my home of MIT in 1949, and he said, "If we are to bring the broad masses of the people in every land to the table of abundance, it can only be by the tireless improvement of all of our means of technical production."

Abraham Lincoln realized there was one other ingredient. He said, "I am a firm believer in the people. If given the truth, they can be depended upon to meet any national crisis. The great point is to give them the plain facts."

So the optimistic note, great point that I want to leave you with is that the plain facts of the machine age are becoming clear, and I have every confidence that we're going to use them to chart a good course into the challenging, abundant economy that we're creating.

Thank you very much.

This is an edited version of McAfee's 2013 TED Talk.
To watch the full talk, visit TED.com.

---

[15] Someone who is "sent to the Gulag" is put in a prison-like environment. Gulags were forced labor camps in Stalin era Russia.

Unit 9 PATRICIA KUHL

The Linguistic Genius of Babies

Part 1

I want you to take a look at this baby. What you're drawn to are her eyes and the skin you love to touch. But today I'm going to talk to you about something you can't see—what's going on up in that little brain of hers. The modern tools of neuroscience are demonstrating to us that what's going on up there is nothing short of rocket science. And what we're learning is going to **shed some light**[1] on what the romantic writers and poets described as the "celestial openness" of the child's mind.

[. . .] Work in my lab is focused on the first critical period in development—and that is the period in which babies try to master which sounds are used in their language. We think, by studying how the sounds are learned, we'll have a model for the rest of language, and perhaps for critical periods that may exist in childhood for social, emotional, and cognitive development. So we've been studying the babies using a technique that we're using all over the world and the sounds of all languages. The baby sits on a parent's lap, and we train them to turn their heads when a sound changes—like from "ah" to "ee." If they do so at the appropriate time, the black box lights up and a panda bear pounds a drum. A **six-monther**[2] adores the task.

What have we learned? Well, babies all over the world are what I like to describe as "citizens of the world." They can discriminate all the sounds of all languages, no matter what country we're testing and what language we're using, and that's remarkable because you and I can't do that. We're culture-bound listeners. We can discriminate the sounds of our own language, but not those of foreign languages. So the question arises: When do those citizens of the world turn into the language-bound listeners that we are? And the answer: before their first birthdays. What you see here is performance on that head-turn task for babies tested in Tokyo and the United States, here in Seattle, as they listened to "ra" and "la"—sounds important to English, but not to Japanese. So at six to eight months, the babies are totally equivalent. Two months later, something incredible occurs. The babies in the United States are getting a lot better, babies in Japan are getting a lot worse, but both of those groups of babies are preparing for exactly the language that they are going to learn.

So the question is: What's happening during this critical two-month period? This is the critical period for sound development, but what's going on up there? So there are two things going on. The first is that the babies are listening intently to us, and they're taking statistics as they listen to us talk—they're taking statistics. So listen to two mothers speaking **motherese**[3]—the universal language we use when we talk to kids—first in English and then in Japanese.

[Video] *English Mother: Ah, I love your big blue eyes—so pretty and nice.*

Japanese Mother: [Japanese]

Part 2

During the production of speech, when babies listen, what they're doing is taking statistics on the language that they

---

[1] To "shed some light" on something means to explain it.

[2] Kuhl refers to a six-month old baby as a "six-monther."

[3] Kuhl uses the expression "motherese" to describe the animated way of speaking to babies that many mothers use.

hear. And those distributions grow. And what we've learned is that babies are sensitive to the statistics, and the statistics of Japanese and English are very, very different. English has a lot of Rs and Ls. The distribution shows. And the distribution of Japanese is totally different, where we see a group of intermediate sounds, which is known as the Japanese "R." So babies absorb the statistics of the language and it changes their brains; it changes them from the citizens of the world to the culture-bound listeners that we are. But we as adults are no longer absorbing those statistics. We're governed by the representations in memory that were formed early in development.

So what we're seeing here is changing our models of what the critical period is about. We're arguing from a mathematical standpoint that the learning of language material may slow down when our distributions stabilize. It's raising lots of questions about bilingual people. Bilinguals must keep two sets of statistics in mind at once and flip between them, one after the other, depending on who they're speaking to.

[. . .] We want to get inside the brain and see this thing happening as babies are in front of televisions, as opposed to in front of human beings. Thankfully, we have a new machine, **magnetoencephalography**[4], that allows us to do this. It looks like a hair dryer from Mars. But it's completely safe, completely **non invasive**[5], and silent. We're looking at millimeter accuracy with regard to spatial and millisecond accuracy using 306 SQUIDs—these are Superconducting QUantum Interference Devices—to pick up the magnetic fields that change as we do our thinking. We're the first in the world to record babies in an MEG machine while they are learning.

So this is little Emma. She's a six-monther. And she's listening to various languages in the earphones that are in her ears. You can see, she can move around. We're tracking her head with little pellets in a cap, so she's free to move completely unconstrained. It's a **technical tour de force**[6]. What are we seeing? We're seeing the baby brain. As the baby hears a word in her language, the auditory areas light up, and then subsequently areas surrounding it that we think are related to coherence, getting the brain coordinated with its different areas, and causality, one brain area causing another to activate.

We are embarking on a grand and golden age of knowledge about child's brain development. We're going to be able to see a child's brain as they experience an emotion, as they learn to speak and read, as they solve a math problem, as they have an idea. And we're going to be able to invent **brain-based interventions**[7] for children who have difficulty learning. Just as the poets and writers described, we're going to be able to see, I think, that wondrous openness, utter and complete openness, of the mind of a child. In investigating the child's brain, we're going to uncover deep truths about what it means to be human, and in the process, we may be able to help keep our own minds open to learning for our entire lives.

This is an edited version of Kuhl's 2011 TED Talk. To watch the full talk, visit TED.com.

---

[4] The magnetoencephalography, or MEG machine, is an apparatus that measures human brain activity by mapping electric currents in the brain. Students can see a picture of it on page 145 of the Student Book.

[5] A device that is "non-invasive" is one that does not go inside the body at all. The MEG machine sits on the child's head, like a helmet.

[6] A synonym for "tour de force" is "masterpiece."

[7] By "brain-based interventions" Kuhl means that new ways to help children with learning disabilities will focus on that child's brain activity while learning.

Innovating to Zero!

Part 1

I'm going to talk today about energy and climate. And that might seem a bit surprising because my full-time work at the **Foundation**[1] is mostly about vaccines and **seeds**[2], about the things that we need to invent and deliver to help the poorest two billion live better lives. But energy and climate are extremely important to these people—in fact, more important than to anyone else on the planet. The climate getting worse means that many years, their crops won't grow: There will be too much rain, not enough rain, things will change in ways that their fragile environment simply can't support. And that leads to starvation, it leads to uncertainty, it leads to unrest. So, the climate changes will be terrible for them.

Also, the price of energy is very important to them. In fact, if you could pick just one thing to lower the price of, to reduce poverty, by far you would pick energy. Now, the price of energy has come down over time. Really advanced civilization is based on advances in energy. The coal revolution fueled the **Industrial Revolution**[3], and, even in the 1900s we've seen a very rapid decline in the price of electricity, and that's why we have refrigerators, air-conditioning, we can make modern materials and do so many things. And so, we're in a wonderful situation with electricity in the rich world. But, as we make it cheaper—and let's go for making it twice as cheap—we need to meet a new constraint, and that constraint **has to do with**[4] CO_2.

CO_2 is warming the planet, and the equation on CO_2 is actually a very straightforward one. If you sum up the CO_2 that gets emitted, that leads to a temperature increase, and that temperature increase leads to some very negative effects: the effects on the weather; perhaps worse, the indirect effects, in that the natural ecosystems can't adjust to these rapid changes, and so you get ecosystem collapses.

Now, the exact amount of how you map from a certain increase of CO_2 to what temperature will be and where the **positive feedbacks**[5] are, there's some uncertainty there, but not very much. And there's certainly uncertainty about how bad those effects will be, but they will be extremely bad. I asked the top scientists on this several times: Do we really have to get down to near zero? Can't we just cut it in half or a quarter? And the answer is that until we get near to zero, the temperature will continue to rise. And so that's a big challenge. It's very different than saying **"We're a twelve-foot-high truck trying to get under a ten-foot bridge, and we can just sort of squeeze under."**[6] This is something that has to get to zero.

Now, we put out a lot of carbon dioxide every year, over 26 billion tons. For each American, it's about 20 tons; for people in poor countries, it's less than one ton. It's an average of about five tons for everyone on the planet. And, somehow, we have to make changes that will bring that down to zero. It's been constantly going up. It's only various economic changes that have even flattened it at all, so we have to go from rapidly rising to falling, and falling all the way to zero.

---

[1] "The Foundation" refers to the Bill & Melinda Gates Foundation.

[2] When Gates mentions "seeds," he is referring to the areas of agriculture that his foundation focuses on helping.

[3] The "Industrial Revolution" refers to the period from the mid-1700s to mid-1800s that saw a new age of manufacturing technology.

[4] If something "has to do with" something else, the two things are related in some way.

[5] The term "positive feedbacks" in regards to climate change refers to something that will increase the effect of the CO_2 emissions.

[6] Gates uses the analogy of a twelve-foot truck and a ten-foot bridge to give an example of a small gap that maybe could be manipulated. Whereas what Gates is talking about, the gap between where carbon emissions are now and zero, is very large and will require a major change in how things are done.

Part 2

This equation has four factors, a little bit of multiplication: So, you've got a thing on the left, CO_2, that you want to get to zero, and that's going to be based on the number of people, the services each person's using on average, the energy on average for each service, and the CO_2 being put out per unit of energy. So let's look at each one of these and see how we can get this down to zero. Probably, one of these numbers is going to have to get pretty near to zero. Now that's back from high school algebra, but let's take a look.

First, we've got population. The world today has 6.8 billion people. That's **headed up**[7] to about nine billion. Now, if we do a really great job on new vaccines, health care, reproductive health services, we could lower that by, perhaps, 10 or 15 percent, but there we see an increase of about 1.3.

The second factor is the services we use. This encompasses everything: the food we eat, clothing, TV, heating. These are very good things: Getting rid of poverty means providing these services to almost everyone on the planet. And it's a great thing for this number to go up. In the rich world, perhaps the top one billion, we probably could cut back and use less, but every year, this number, on average, is going to go up, and so, overall, that will more than double the services delivered per person. Here we have a very basic service: Do you have lighting in your house to be able to read your homework? And, in fact, these kids don't, so they're going out and reading their schoolwork under the street lamps.

Now, efficiency, E, the energy for each service, here finally we have some good news. We have something that's not going up. Through various inventions and new ways of doing lighting, through different types of cars, different ways of building buildings—there are a lot of services where you can bring the energy for that service down quite substantially. Some individual services even bring it down by 90 percent. There are other services like how we make fertilizer, or how we do air transport, where the rooms for improvement are far, far less. And so, overall here, if we're optimistic, we may get a reduction of a factor of three to even, perhaps, a factor of six. But for these first three factors now, we've gone from 26 billion to, at best, maybe 13 billion tons, and that just won't cut it.

So let's look at this fourth factor—this is going to be a key one—and this is the amount of CO_2 put out per each unit of energy. And so the question is: Can you actually get that to zero? If you burn coal, no. If you burn natural gas, no. Almost every way we make electricity today, except for the emerging renewables and nuclear, puts out CO_2. And so, what we're going to have to do **at a global scale**[8], is create a new system. And so, we need energy miracles.

Now, when I use the term "miracle," I don't mean something that's impossible. The microprocessor is a miracle. The personal computer is a miracle. The Internet and its services are a miracle. So the people here have participated in the creation of many miracles. Usually, we don't have a deadline, where you have to get the miracle by a certain date. Usually,

---

[7] In regards to numbers, something that is "headed up" is increasing.

[8] When something happens on "a global scale," it affects the entire world.

you just kind of stand by, and some come along, some don't. This is a case where we actually have to **drive at full speed**[9] and get a miracle in a pretty tight timeline.

Part 3

[. . .] So let's think: How should we measure ourselves? What should our **report card**[10] look like? Well, let's go out to where we really need to get, and then look at the intermediate. For 2050, you've heard many people talk about this 80 percent reduction. That really is very important, that we get there. And that 20 percent will be used up by things going on in poor countries, still some agriculture, hopefully we will have cleaned up forestry, cement. So to get to that 80 percent, the developed countries, including countries like China, will have had to switch their electricity generation altogether. So, the other grade is: Are we deploying this zero-emission technology, have we deployed it in all the developed countries and we're in the process of getting it elsewhere? That's super important. That's a key element of making that report card.

So, **backing up**[11] from there, what should the 2020 report card look like? Well, again, it should have the two elements. We should go through these efficiency measures to start getting reductions: The less we emit, the less that sum will be of CO_2, and, therefore, the less the temperature. But in some ways, the grade we get there, doing things that don't get us all the way to the big reductions, is only equally, or maybe even slightly less, important than the other, which is the pace of innovation on these breakthroughs.

[. . .] So this is a wish. It's a very **concrete**[12] wish that we invent this technology. If you gave me only one wish for the next 50 years—I could pick who's president, I could pick a vaccine, which is something I love, or I could pick that this thing that's half the cost with no CO_2 gets invented—this is the wish I would pick. This is the one with the greatest impact. If we don't get this wish, the division between the people who think short term and long term will be terrible, between the U.S. and China, between poor countries and rich, and most of all the lives of those two billion will be far worse.

So what do we have to do? What am I appealing to you to step forward and drive? We need to go for more research funding. When countries get together in places like Copenhagen, they shouldn't just discuss the CO_2. They should discuss this innovation agenda, and you'd be stunned at the ridiculously low levels of spending on these innovative approaches. We do need the market incentives—CO_2 tax, cap and trade—something that gets that price signal out there. We need to get the message out. We need to have this dialogue be a more rational, more understandable dialogue, including the steps that the government takes. This is an important wish, but it is one I think we can achieve.

This is an edited version of Gates's 2010 TED Talk. To watch the full talk, visit TED.com.

---

[9] Gates uses the metaphor "drive at full speed" to illustrate that we are moving quickly in the direction of extreme environmental damage due to carbon emissions and global warming.

[10] A "report card" refers to the grades that students get at the end of a school year in the U.S.

[11] The term "backing up" is used by Gates here to indicate that he is moving backwards on the time line he is talking about, from 2050 to 2020.

[12] When an idea or wish is described as "concrete," it means it is specific and fixed.

Credits

Acknowledgements

The Authors and Publisher would like to thank the following teaching professionals for their valuable input during the development of this series:

Coleeta Paradise Abdullah, Certified Training Center; **Wilder Yesid Escobar Almeciga,** Universidad El Bosque; **Tara Amelia Arntsen,** Northern State University; **Mei-ho Chiu,** Soochow University; **Amy Cook,** Bowling Green State University; **Anthony Sean D'Amico,** SDH Institute; **Mariel Doyenart,** Alianza Cultural Uruguay-Estados Unidos; **Raichle Farrelly,** American University of Armenia; **Douglas E. Forster,** Japan Women's University; **Rosario Giraldez,** Alianza Cultural Uruguay-Estados Unidos; **Floyd H. Graham III,** Kansai Gaidai University; **Jay Klaphake,** Kyoto University of Foreign Studies; **Anthony G. Lavigne,** Kansai Gaidai University; **Adriana Castañeda Londoño,** Centro Colombo Americano; **Alexandra Dylan Lowe,** SUNY Westchester Community College; **Elizabeth Ortiz Lozada,** COPEI - COPOL English Institute; **David Matijasevich,** Canadian Education College; **Jennie Popp,** Universidad Andrés Bello; **Ubon Pun-ubon,** Sripatum University; **Yoko Sakurai,** Aichi University; **Michael J. Sexton,** PSB Academy; **Jenay Seymour,** Hongik University; **Karenne Sylvester,** New College Manchester; **Mark S. Turnoy; Hajime Uematsu,** Hirosaki University; **Nae-Dong Yang,** National Taiwan University.